THE WALL STREET JOURNAL.

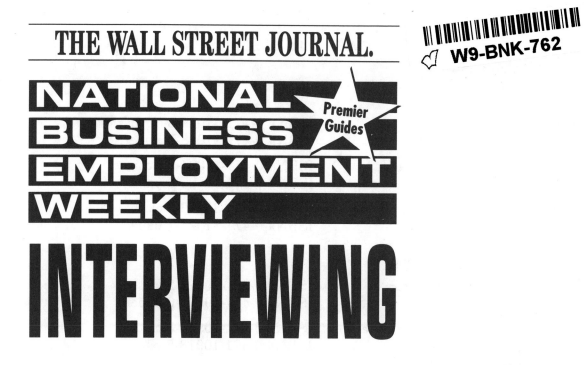

NATIONAL BUSINESS EMPLOYMENT WEEKLY

Premier Guides

INTERVIEWING

W9-BNK-762

THE NATIONAL BUSINESS EMPLOYMENT WEEKLY
PREMIER GUIDES SERIES

<u>Published:</u>

Resumes,	ISBN# 0-471-31029-8 cloth; ISBN# 0-471-31028-X paper
Interviewing,	ISBN# 0-471-31024-7 cloth; ISBN# 0-471-31025-5 paper
Networking,	ISBN# 0-471-31026-3 cloth; ISBN# 0-471-31027-1 paper

<u>Forthcoming:</u>

Cover Letters,	ISBN# 0-471-10671-2 cloth; ISBN# 0-471-10672-0 paper
Alternative Careers,	ISBN# 0-471-10919-3 cloth; ISBN# 0-471-10918-5 paper

THE WALL STREET JOURNAL.

NATIONAL BUSINESS EMPLOYMENT WEEKLY

Premier Guides

INTERVIEWING

Arlene S. Hirsch

John Wiley & Sons, Inc.
New York • Chichester • Brisbane • Toronto • Singapore

National Business Employment Weekly and *The Wall Street Journal* are registered trademarks of Dow Jones & Company, Inc.

This text is printed on acid-free paper.

Copyright © 1994 by National Business Employment Weekly
Published by John Wiley & Sons, Inc.

All rights reserved. Published simultaneously in Canada.

Reproduction or translation of any part of this work beyond that permitted by Section 107 or 108 of the 1976 United States Copyright Act without the permission of the copyright owner is unlawful. Requests for permission or further information should be addressed to the Permissions Department, John Wiley & Sons, Inc., 605 Third Avenue, New York, NY 10158-0012.

This publication is designed to provide accurate and authoritative information in regard to the subject matter covered. It is sold with the understanding that the publisher is not engaged in rendering legal, accounting, or other professional services. If legal advice or other expert assistance is required, the services of a competent professional person should be sought.

Library of Congress Cataloging in Publication Data:

National Business Employment Weekly.
    Interviewing / by National Business Employment Weekly.
        p.   cm.
    Includes bibliographical references.
    ISBN 0-471-31024-7 (cloth : acid-free paper). — ISBN
0-471-31025-5 (pbk.)
    1. Employment interviewing—United States. 2. Job hunting—United
States. I. National business employment weekly. II. Title.
III. Title: Guide to interviewing.
  HF5549.5.I6H57   1994
  650.14—dc20   94-329

Printed in the United States of America

10 9 8 7 6 5

To my parents,
with love

Foreword

No job-search activity creates greater stress among candidates than interviewing. Having to impress strangers enough for them to hire you is a daunting task. What if they ask a question you can't answer? Perhaps they want to know specific details about an embarrassing mistake, or probe to uncover career aspirations you've never shared with anyone.

At some point in your search, you'll have to perform on cue in an interview. Knowing what to say and how to say it is critical, as is having a complete understanding of the employer's needs. Determining what you want in a new position is important as well, and career counselor Arlene Hirsch does a terrific job of explaining how you can handle these issues with confidence.

Arlene starts by outlining what employers look for when interviewing applicants. She offers an easy-to-remember format that will help you prepare for even the toughest interviewers, then follows it up with a long list of questions you'll most likely be asked, and provides some suggested responses.

What makes Arlene's approach unique is her explanation of some usually well-hidden aspects of the process. She explains the psychology of interviewing (including how to "psych yourself up"), the body language you can expect to see, and guidelines for dealing with the unusual when it arises. She also covers the types of questions you should be ready to ask, and the steps necessary to follow up effectively, both the next day and beyond.

Finally, Arlene tackles several issues that are more important than ever in a global economy, such as working with international headhunters and interviewing with hiring managers who represent foreign companies. She also provides advice on negotiating the best pay package once you have an offer in hand.

To be sure, every interview situation is different. But by reading this book, you'll gain a complete understanding of what employers want to hear when you meet face to face.

TONY LEE
Editor
National Business Employment Weekly

Acknowledgments

Writing a book can be an isolating experience but, for me, it's also been a journey of connection. I'm particularly indebted to those friends and colleagues who so generously shared their time, insights and stories: Laurie Anderson, Pat Berg, Linda Bougie, Liz Branstead, Phyllis Edelen, Rick Ehlers, Roger Gilman, Jerry Hannigan, Cheryl Heisler, Debbie Holdstein, Jim Kacena, Mary Ann Lee, Bob Maher, Joy Reed-Belt, Monica Tulley and Tom Washington, to mention a few.

Books need editors, and mine has been blessed with many. My gratitude to *National Business Employment Weekly* editors Gabrielle Solomon—whose painstaking attention to detail and cheerful personality made the partnership more pleasurable; and to Tony Lee, who first recognized my writing talent and continues to honor me with "plum assignments" for the *NBEW*.

Special thanks to cartoonist Tom Cheney for his wonderful contributions to this book.

Extra special thanks to my sister, Nancy Hirsch. Her generous spirit and boundless love and support are always appreciated and deserve more credit.

About the Author

Arlene Hirsch is a career counselor, psychotherapist and outplacement consultant in Chicago. Since launching her practice more than 10 years ago, she's worked with a diverse population of individuals and corporations, helping to address their career planning, development and management needs. She also presents workshops and seminars, and frequently serves as a guest speaker to groups and on radio and television. Ms. Hirsch received a bachelor's degree in English from the University of Iowa, and a master's degree in counseling psychology from Northwestern University. She currently teaches at DePaul University's School for New Learning in Chicago.

Contents

"Wow! Talk about thorough interviews!"

Introduction

When Monica Tulley was looking for her first sales position, she agreed to meet an interviewer at a local Pizza Hut restaurant. No sooner had they parked themselves in a corner booth than the interviewer took off his wristwatch, handed it to Tulley and commanded her, "Sell me this watch."

Like many eager-to-please interviewees, Tulley, now an international marketing manager in Cleveland, did her best to comply. She stumbled through an inept and halfhearted sales pitch, which apparently didn't work because she didn't get the job.

With 20-20 hindsight, a more experienced and self-confident Tulley realizes that she should have handled the entire situation differently. "You can't sell a product without product knowledge," she says. "I should have asked for more information about the features and benefits of the watch, not to mention its intended market. Then, I could have formulated a thoughtful sales strategy and sold it to him properly."

Like many interviewees, Tulley was intimidated by the employer's aggressive style. She backed off when she would have been better served by adopting a relationship-selling approach. In relationship selling, the job hunter takes the initiative to probe for the buyer's needs. After all, it doesn't make sense to start selling before you have some idea of what the buyer will buy.

Throughout this book, I emphasize the importance of "relationship goals": What you say counts, but the context within which you say it often counts more. As we begin to formulate answers to many of the typical questions employers like to ask prospective new hires, we'll frequently return to the myriad ways in which you can frame your responses to enhance your conversations.

Although the standard question-answer format used by many interviewers can prompt the feeling that you've walked into a combat zone, there are many ways to level the playing field. One possibility is to take the initiative. Introduce a question-answer-question format in which you answer the question that was asked, then follow up with a related question of your own.

For example, you can close your response to the anxiety-provoking "tell me about yourself" question by saying "Now that I've told you about myself, can you tell me more about the position?" Or, after responding to a question like "How do you handle authority?" finish up with "Can you tell me something about how you like to manage people?"

This approach equalizes the relationship so that it feels more like two adult human beings having a conversation. In the process, it also accomplishes what should be one of your primary objectives of interviewing: to determine whether this is a good job for you.

Many executives feel so uncomfortable and insecure as interviewees that they lose sight of how they might better manage the process. Many experts liken interviewing to courtship and marriage. When things go right, the end result is the same: A successful relationship has been established. This analogy helps place the interview within a different context. If successful, it's the beginning of a relationship with an employer who will someday become your employment mate. Therefore, it's imperative that you take the initiative not only to sell yourself but to make sure that you're buying into a relationship that's really good for you. Otherwise, you'll greatly increase the likelihood of an untimely professional divorce.

Good relationships (professional or otherwise) are built on mutual trust, respect and admiration. Interviews (format notwithstanding) are no exception to this rule. Sometimes, the toughest challenge you'll face involves achieving a more equal footing with your potential employer.

Jerry Hannigan, a former product manager with American Telephone & Telegraph Co., learned this lesson when interviewing with the owner of a manufacturing company in Illinois. On paper, Hannigan's revenue-producing credentials were impressive. His resume showed that in less than four years, he had boosted revenues fivefold on all 11 of his AT&T products. He should have been the answer to this employer's marketing prayers.

But the interviewer didn't really question Hannigan about his marketing accomplishments, even though he was clear about wanting and needing someone who could produce results and revenues quickly. Instead, noting that the applicant's resume indicated an ability to speak French, the interviewer asked him to translate a sentence from a French text. The phrase (which Hannigan translated) read: "Don't promise what you can't deliver."

We can only speculate as to this interviewer's motives, but evidently, he was skeptical that Hannigan was the real thing. Or, perhaps he'd been burned before by applicants who promised results they couldn't deliver. In either case, the interviewer explored this candidate's credibility and qualifications in a cockeyed fashion. Had he really wanted to assure himself of Hannigan's abilities, he should have tested him with a hypothetical marketing situation, not a translation.

Unfortunately, Hannigan got so caught up in trying to demonstrate his French language skills (and felt so relieved when he passed) that he, too, missed the essential point. After passing the interviewer's test, he should have explored the reasons behind it. By probing deeply for concerns, he might have reassured the employer more directly and thereby won himself a job offer.

The way an employer conducts an interview can tell astute interviewees a lot about the organization. While interviewing for a senior organizational development position with four senior executives (over lunch), management consultant Richard Silverman was bombarded by questions from all directions. Fortunately, he felt equal to the challenge of the barrage, although he did slow down the questioning by thinking carefully before providing each answer. When it was over, he had a few questions of his own.

"Basically, I wanted to know about their priorities for the position," he says. "When they came up with a list of 16 high-priority items, my suspicions were confirmed. The job was undoable. They were just too disorganized."

Silverman suggests that interviewees develop a new mind-set. "Picture yourself more like a consultant. In that role, your job is to find out the employer's problems, then present solutions."

Los Angeles career consultant Bob McCarthy agrees. "Rather than thinking of yourself as a job hunter looking for a job, think of yourself as a solution to a problem."

Although many interviewees tend to cast themselves in the role of a beggar looking for a handout, interviewers seldom hire people out of the goodness of their hearts. They're looking for people who can solve business problems. A candidate who understands what those problems are—and offers a method of solving them—will land the most job offers.

Taking an active stance has lots of other benefits, too. It helps you manage your anxiety and present your best professional self. It also allows you to evaluate objectively whether you really want to play on that employment team. This mental shift requires a healthy dose of self-esteem. You aren't a criminal on trial for your livelihood or a mediocre sales representative with a second-rate product, you're someone with critical skills who can add value to the right organization.

People who have been fired or laid off may have more trouble adopting this perspective. To do so can require some "emotional homework" in the form of resolving feelings and regaining equilibrium. If you can learn to treat the interview as a learning process, it can facilitate that goal rather than undermine it.

A laid-off construction engineer was tripped up by the question, "How do you handle authority?" Suddenly, his whole childhood with an abusive stepfather welled up inside him, and before he knew what he was saying, he responded, "I don't." (Fortunately, he was in therapy to deal with the problem and was able to understand where his answer came from, so that he would not repeat his mistake with another potential employer.)

Just as there are imperfect interviewers, there are no perfect interview candidates. How can there be, since interviewing is an imperfect transaction between human beings?

This book will show you how to remove some of the negative imagery from the interviewing process by developing better interview skills and attitudes. You should have plenty of incentive. No sane employer will want to hire you if you view yourself as a lamb headed for the slaughterhouse.

Your task is threefold:

1. Get to know your product (yourself) inside out.

2. Research customers (employers) who are most likely to buy that product.

3. Present your product as something that can really add value to an organization.

Follow this formula and I promise that you'll find job-search success much faster and more effectively than is otherwise possible—while also doing wonders for your self-esteem.

"Of course, you realize that this position will force you to confront your problem with shyness."

1

What Employers Look For

J ob hunters learn quickly that the candidates who get offers aren't always those who most closely match the stated hiring requirements. So if you can't trust job descriptions, how can you determine what employers really want?

The truth is, most hiring managers want pretty much the same thing: the *safest* candidate they can find.

"Employers aren't always sure what they're looking for, but they always want to minimize the risk," says an Indianapolis outplacement consultant. "If you can help them do that, they'll hire you."

Says Pat Engler-Parish, Vice President of Aspen Software, a Laramie, Wyoming company, which develops interviewing tools for employers:

Employers are always searching for a magic pill. An easy solution to the selection process. But the truth is, there's no easy prescription. It takes a lot of hard work to get it right.

Why are executives so afraid of selecting the wrong candidate?

☆ **Hiring Mistakes Are Expensive.** Experts estimate that hiring mistakes cost American businesses $100 billion per year—money that could obviously be spent in better ways.

☆ **Hiring Mistakes Cost Influence.** A hiring manager who can't hire (or keep) good people loses credibility with bosses, co-workers and underlings. Nobody thinks poor social judgment is admirable.

☆ **Hiring Mistakes Cost Time and Energy.** No manager wants to go through the time-consuming hiring (and subsequent training) process unnecessarily. It takes time, energy and attention away from other important activities.

To overcome employers' inherent fears and doubts, you don't have to come across like a cheerleader or a workaholic. You just have to develop enough professional rapport during interviews to allay their fears of making a hiring mistake. You should also try to show that you fit the following profile of a low-risk hire:

1. Someone who wants to do the job and won't leave soon.

2. Someone who will fit in.

3. Someone who's likable.

4. Someone with the skills to do the job.

5. Someone who will work hard to pursue the organization's goals.

6. Someone who will make the employer look good.

Most employers are afraid of job-hoppers. Because it takes time and energy to hire and train new employees, they don't want to be a mere stepping-stone in your career climb. This means that your interests and career goals must match what they have to offer.

A construction manager who wanted to move off the management track into a more hands-on role had to work hard to persuade employers that he'd truly be happy in a job for which he seemed overqualified. He did so, convincingly, by describing his favorite projects and embellishing the hands-on role he had played in each.

In another scenario, a personal injury attorney had worked for a half-dozen different firms in 12 years of practice. Her challenge was to convince prospective employers that for them, she'd stick around longer.

She couldn't argue that point successfully without (1) identifying common threads of discontent in her career history and (2) determining whether these firms really would be different from previous employers. Reviewing her experience, she realized that she'd always been the sole female professional at the firms she'd worked for and that she was tired of her role as "token woman."

Thus, she began prequalifying employers before applying to them. By eliminating male-only firms from her list, she was able to speak more openly about her needs and desires in interviews. She also was able to select the firms she genuinely wanted to work for, rather than simply joining whichever employer happened to offer her a job.

The best way to convince employers that you really want to do the job is, in fact, to actually want to do the job. A little self-assessment—or soul-searching—will help you accomplish that goal. Unless you have great acting skills, faking enthusiasm rarely works.

Show That You Will Fit into the Work Environment

A recently promoted regional manager for a contract furnishings company found that his supervisory style antagonized two of his new sales representatives. Within six months, both representatives were gone. After that, the manager was deathly afraid that if he hired the wrong replacements, his reputation with the company would be seriously jeopardized.

In such a highly charged situation, it's hard for candidates to prove their worth. Fortunately, one prospective sales representative had the foresight to ask the interviewer what had happened to the previous incumbent. It soon became clear that the manager felt threatened by representatives who liked working independently.

As it turned out, the candidate was used to being closely supervised. Thus, he made a point of focusing on the comfortable relationship he had with his former boss—a hands-on manager who liked to be involved in the details of his employees' activities. This proved to be just the kind of reassurance the hiring manager needed, and the candidate got an offer.

Some interviewers may be more concerned about other issues of personality fit. When Ed Goedert, president of a psychological testing firm in Oakbrook, Illinois, interviews candidates, he's primarily concerned with three aspects of their personal style:

1. He evaluates candidates' communication skills. Rather than examining their capacity to talk endlessly, Goedert looks for the ability to organize thoughts clearly and concisely, and to listen and respond sensitively.

2. He considers candidates' nonverbal communication. Interviewees who are dressed inappropriately, display poor social judgment, are excessively anxious, or aren't well-groomed lose considerable points.

3. He analyzes their work habits. Is the candidate a perfectionist? A workaholic? A hip shooter? Then, more importantly, he considers how the individual's style fits in with his client's corporate culture. If there's a match, it's more likely the candidate will win a job offer.

Be Likable

A talented systems administrator for a computer software company lost his job when the facility closed down. During his search, he was lucky enough to have a former boss who was willing to praise his performance enthusiastically. Unfortunately, potential employers never bothered to check the administrator's references because they couldn't get past his low-key communication style.

During interviews, he often provided one-sentence answers. This "silent treatment" intimidated interviewers and made them uneasy. Rather than deal with the psychological discomfort or try to draw the candidate out, employers filled the silence with their own chatter. Then, they'd decide not to pursue his candidacy further.

To combat this problem, the systems administrator had to make an active, conscious effort to open up. He decided to use personal information to demonstrate that he was a mature, stable and community-minded individual, not a reclusive isolationist. For example, he began telling employers that he was a lifelong resident of his community, married and actively involved with his two children.

He also tried harder to elaborate on responses to interviewers' queries. He started using more anecdotes and began following up with more questions of his own. These steps warmed the interview atmosphere considerably and, in turn, helped him feel more comfortable with the process.

Have the Skills to Do the Job

Robert Maher, a senior consultant in the Dallas office of outplacement firm Lee Hecht Harrison, likes to use a bell-curve diagram to illustrate hiring companies' priorities.

"The majority of employers fall into the 'fat part' of the bell curve, which means that they interview primarily to a candidate's knowledge, skills and experience," says Maher. (At either extreme of the diagram, you will find employers with a well-considered candidate profile that includes issues of character and values and employers who don't have a clue about what they need.)

This concern about candidates' raw ability makes sense: "Jobs are designed to accomplish a specific result so, obviously, it's important to know whether a candidate has the skills and experience to achieve that result," says Marianne Ruggiero, senior vice-president of human resources for GFT USA Corporation in New York.

Misjudging a candidate's skills can have serious consequences for both parties. The owner of a construction company hired a new manager who, during the interview process, seemed quite able: He had solid academic credentials, had worked for two of the company's competitors and knew the industry well. The manager never mentioned, however, that he'd been asked to resign from his two previous positions because of insufficient management skills. The resulting third termination left hard feelings on both sides.

Such bad experiences are why employers are leery of candidates who "talk a good game." Unless you can back up assertions with evidence and good references, don't expect hiring managers to believe your sales pitch.

A facilities manager proved his accomplishments by creating an impressive portfolio that showcased his achievements. It contained sets of before-and-after photographs, arranged by project, for a series of renovations he had coordinated. It also included letters of recommendation from satisfied clients. This visual documentation gave potential employers an objective feel for the quality of his work.

Be Ready to Work Hard to Pursue the Organization's Goals

"Companies may give lip service to the idea that they want every candidate to be honest, truthful and nice to their mother," says Ruggiero, "but what they really want are people who are going to work hard—people who have the will, motivation and interest in working."

So while you may work primarily for the paycheck, you're better off keeping that information to yourself. Employers believe that employees who work because they sincerely believe in what they do will be the most diligent. Thus, they prefer to hire candidates who are dedicated to the organization's objectives and who really want to play on their team.

"I'm impressed with a candidate who says to me, 'No one will work harder or make a greater commitment to your mission,'" says Ken Freeman, manager of employee relations at Dartmouth College in Hanover, New Hampshire.

FOR YOUR INFORMATION

A SPECTRUM OF CORPORATE VALUES

A wide range of values can be found among different employers. In the growing field of biotechnology, for example, creativity, innovative thinking and love of a challenge are highly prized. In the hospitality industry, dedication to customer service and sociability rank higher on the list of preferred attributes. And in the nonprofit sector, commitment to the cause outweighs pure fiscal ability.

Your best bet, then, is to target employers and industries whose values match your strengths.

Make the Employer Look Good

It may seem self-serving, but managers naturally prefer to hire employees who'll improve their own standing in the organization.

Consider the case of an administrator with a social services agency in Chicago who was looking for an office manager. She'd thought about hiring someone from the private sector for the job, but wasn't convinced it would be a good idea.

Yet when a candidate described how a bottom-line mentality could enable the agency to deliver more services, she began to realize the benefit of choosing a manager who came from a business background, rather than a social-work background.

The administrator knew her choice might initially be unpopular (especially among social workers). However, she was confident that the candidate's skills (and eventual accomplishments) would make her department stand out favorably. The administrator hoped this would demonstrate her vision, leadership and courage to the rest of the management team.

As you can see from this example, you don't have to have a perfectly synchronized history of goals and accomplishments to link up with employers. But you do need to show some emotional logic and maturity regarding the career decisions you've made.

While employers are inclined to view past history as the best predictor of future success, losses can be recouped and direction changed. Your attitude may prove the crucial variable.

The ability to live with (and learn from) your mistakes and choices will go a long way toward convincing employers to accept them (and you), too.

"First of all, I'd like to dispel any rumors you may have heard about our company's financial difficulties . . ."

2

The Art and Skill of Preparation

The acronym R E A S O N describes a six-step process of interview preparation: researching the company, establishing selling points, anticipating objections, storytelling, organizing yourself and negotiating. Once you're familiar with these elements, focus your attention on those areas that are most important for your specific situation.

Research the Company

Mickey Allweiss, a partner in the growing New Orleans law firm of Lowe, Stein, Hoffman, Allweiss & Hauver, needed to fill a position for a new associate. Two candidates stood out in his mind for their failure to master two simple facts: The firm has the largest domestic practice in the state and Allweiss is a litigator who maintains some distance from the domestic practice.

The first lawyer-candidate had his heart (and career goals) set on practicing admiralty law. Lowe, Stein et al. doesn't handle any admiralty cases. Had the candidate known that, he would have saved everyone the wasted interview time and effort.

The second lawyer-candidate was closer (but still no cigar). He was interested in practicing domestic law. Since the firm is known for its domestic practice, he was definitely in the right place. But he was talking to the wrong person.

Both candidates would have needed to do only the most minimal research to avoid their errors. "All they had to do was look us up in the Martindale-Hubbell Directory to find out what the members of the firm specialize in," says Allweiss. "It isn't that hard."

Candidates who arrive at interviews so completely unprepared are remembered for all the wrong reasons. Instead of showcasing their competence and thoroughness, they display a seat-of-the-pants mentality that doesn't do much to win employers' favor.

Most good research begins—but doesn't necessarily end—at the public library or information center. To make your time there most effective, it usually makes sense to seek out a reference librarian who is familiar with the resources, explain the purpose of your research, and ask for assistance.

But don't expect the public library to be the be-all and end-all of your research. No single location is likely to have everything you need. Time permitting, you might also want to check with government offices, professional associations and specialized libraries for more detailed information.

Before you start burrowing around in the stacks, however, give some thought to what kind of information you really need to prepare yourself for the interview. Ideally, that information will help you prepare tailored responses to some of the more standard questions *and* unearth potential areas of concern that might require further discussion and exploration.

When a media relations professional was granted an interview with the communications director of a prestigious Chicago museum, she buried herself in the library for a whole day studying past newspaper and magazine coverage of the institution. And since media coverage was her bailiwick, this allowed her to better understand the actual responsibilities of the position she'd be expected to handle.

In the process, she discovered some interesting factual discrepancies in reports. This tipped her off to an "accuracy of information" problem that had been frustrating and undermining the department head. Knowing these facts changed

FOR YOUR INFORMATION

THE VALUE OF RESEARCH

1. It gives focus to an interview strategy.
2. It enables you to make a better presentation.
3. It conveys interest and enthusiasm to potential employers.
4. It demonstrates thoroughness, competence and emotional readiness to work.
5. It enhances your ability to make an informed decision.
6. It encourages you to make choices.

the whole tenor of the conversation, leading the director to remark, "You really do your homework, don't you?"

In *Researching Your Way to a Good Job* (Wiley, 1993), business librarian Karmen Crowther suggests that interviewees search out the following types of information about companies:

Location

Facilities

Size

Products/Services

Financial Data

History

Strategies and Goals

Management and Employee Data

Executive Biography

However revealing this information may be, keep in mind that printed materials become quickly outdated. As a result, you may want to supplement those sources with electronic database information.

You may also find that you have more difficulty uncovering information about small local or regional companies. People are always good sources of supplementary information. Whenever possible, tap into your personal network of contacts for some behind-the-scenes information about the target company. You can also look to the company's competitors, suppliers and customers for the "inside scoop." Finally, don't be afraid to ask the employer directly to provide you with information that might prove helpful in preparing for the interview. Brochures, marketing materials, annual reports and job descriptions can be enormously beneficial.

Research alone, of course, represents no magical solution. It must be translated into an effective interviewing strategy, which brings me to my next point.

Establish Selling Points

The more closely your selling points reflect your employer's buying points, the better chance you have of closing the deal.

Once you've done your preliminary research into a company, you're in a better position to establish your best selling points.

When "Paul," a former corporate travel manager, finessed an interview for a sales position with a luxurious hotel chain, he was able to use his wide base of business contacts to obtain inside information about the organization. After learning that they hoped to target the growing Chicago tourism and convention business, he realized that his skill at building new sales territories would probably be of great interest to this employer. By coupling that with the fact that he already had a plethora of Chicago business contacts, he hoped to clinch the deal.

A selling point is a marketable skill or personal quality that can be succinctly stated. Paul's would be "I can develop new sales territories" and "I have many useful business contacts in the Chicago community."

Marketable skills can be divided into three areas:

1. Technical qualifications (e.g., "I can program in 'C' language").

2. General liberal arts skills ("I have good verbal and written communication skills," "I'm a good problem-solver").

3. Character traits ("I'm dependable," "I'm resourceful," "I'm a very hard worker").

Former operations analyst Mary Lou Johnson planned to use general skills developed through her professional work and as her church's social chair to transition into the hospitality industry, either as a concierge or meeting planner.

FOR YOUR INFORMATION

TAP INTO TRANSFERABLE SKILLS

"Interviewees should take a broad approach when thinking about their marketable skills," says Ingrid Murro Botero, president of Phoenix-based Murro Consulting. "Informal knowledge also counts. You don't just learn at work. Education and volunteer activities provide lots of informal knowledge that can also be marketable."

Her list of selling points included that she was well organized, customer service oriented ("I see service as a privilege"), and quality conscious. Having learned her previous position from the ground floor up, she considered herself very "teachable." In addition, she worked well under pressure, was always willing to go the extra mile and liked a challenge.

Most job search experts agree that it's crucial for candidates to have a clear understanding of the skills and accomplishments they like to convey to future employers.

The emphasis is often on quantifiable results and identifiable outcomes which demonstrate the quality and effectiveness of the candidate's work performance. Any time you saved your employer time or money, increased profits or productivity, initiated and/or implemented programs or systems or in any other way demonstrated your value to the company, you have a bona fide selling point.

Awards, bonuses and performance evaluations can provide some of the objective data you need to document your skills; but if you're unable to discuss your achievements directly, most employers will never get to that information.

Accomplishments don't have to be monumental to count. In the new workplace spirit of "team play," your overall contribution to your team's efforts can go a long way.

Range may be as important as depth. People who have a diverse skill set may find themselves with a proverbial "leg up" in the marketplace. Why? Because it shows a flexibility that's highly valued in today's constantly changing work climate. It also gives you the opportunity to present yourself to potential employers in a variety of different ways since you'll discover that different employers have different needs and goals.

In my own case, for example, I've discovered that I have six major areas of skills and accomplishments: marketing/public relations, project management, teaching/training, writing, counseling and consulting. What I choose to emphasize obviously depends on the nature of the position I'm applying for.

For more ideas about how this process works, please read Chapter 3: "Typical Questions."

Anticipate Objections

It isn't enough to know your strengths. You must also know your weaknesses so you can prepare an effective defense. Chapter 4, "Red Flags," should enable you to better understand and handle employer objections without getting defensive. As you read, think about which questions and issues pose the greatest concern for you. Then script out responses that put the best face on the truth.

For example, when interviewing in new industries, veteran product manager Jerry Hannigan describes the fresh perspective he can bring to that industry as a result of his diverse background. In other words, he argues that not being an industry specialist is an advantage.

Value is in the eye of the beholder. The degree to which a buyer's needs match your product's qualities determines its value in that particular arena. Sometimes, though, convincing employers of your value requires a tough sell.

When Governors State University professor Deborah Holdstein interviewed for a brand management position with Procter & Gamble, she found herself battling stereotypes surrounding her PhD in English.

"I'm worried about this 'ivory tower' thing," one senior manager told her. "I'm afraid you won't be practical enough. You'll be too theoretical."

Holdstein proceeded to launch into something of a tirade about the ultimate practicality of her humanities skills.

"I can analyze problems, organize information and communicate solutions. My job is to make sense out of complex information," Holdstein says. "Now, tell me what could be more practical than that?"

"Besides," she adds dryly, "good theories can be practical, too. That's why people at Harvard Business School teach them with case studies."

After she calmed down, Holdstein realized that the employer had expressed an honest concern, and she'd risen to the competitive challenge.

"I wasn't sure I wanted the job," she says. "But I knew that I wanted to win." (When the offer came through a short hour later, she knew she'd succeeded.)

In the meantime, though, she'd acquired a few reservations of her own. While talking with another brand manager (whose function was to sell her on the company), she learned that P&G was having trouble selling its 48-ounce Ivory soap product.

The marketing manager was very proud that he'd developed a marketing plan to shrink-wrap romance novels with the soap in order to "entice overweight women in curlers with kids hanging out of their grocery carts" to buy the product.

"The guy's attitude toward the buyer was offensive," Holdstein says. "And while I have to admit the romance novels were a good marketing idea, I didn't think I'd be happy in that environment. I was actually happier in academe."

Storytelling

It isn't enough to say "I can do this" or "I'm good at that." You have to prove it. Storytelling is a great way to anchor your selling points with proof.

"Aloof as they may seem, employers are actually begging you to get them excited. Show that you can make or save them money, solve their operational problems or ease their workloads and they'll be thrilled to hire you," says Tom Washington, president of Career Management Resources in Bellevue, Washington. "Merely saying you can increase productivity or get staff members to work as a team isn't enough. You must support your claims with vivid examples."

Using anecdotal evidence to describe your job skills is a highly effective interview technique. In a few short minutes, you can tell a powerful story that will encourage interviewers to remember you months later.

Washington remembers tracking down a woman he'd interviewed seven months earlier because she'd impressed him with stories about the client base she'd developed, which was loaded with referrals and repeat customers.

Stories are effective because they provide concrete examples of how people perform in real-life situations. They're a lively way to showcase your skills and make a strong impact on hiring managers.

But they must be carefully chosen. An experienced litigation attorney remembers one time when his proverbial storytelling charm misfired. Thinking that his interviewer's name was Don Brown, he spent the first 10 minutes of his interview raving on about "Don Brown's Candy Store," which was just around the corner from his home.

The interviewer listened and said nothing.

Several months later, the attorney found out his interviewer's name was Don Braun. How much this influenced the fact that Don Braun didn't extend him a job offer will never be known, but it certainly couldn't have helped.

(In Chapter 5, "Not-So-Typical Questions," you'll find lots of helpful tips on how to develop an effective storyline and prepare a repertoire of good stories with which to sell yourself.)

Psychologist Laurie Anderson goes one step further in her approach to storytelling. "It's not enough to tell a good story," Anderson says. "You have to let employers know why you're telling them that particular story."

She suggests leading with a very direct approach: "I tell you this because . . ."

It may not be subtle, but it does make for strong, clear communication.

Organize Yourself

You can create an impression of competence by the way you manage interview logistics. This includes making sure you present a good visual image. Good grooming counts.

"Physicality matters whether we want it to or not," says Mickey Allweiss. "When I assess potential associates for my firm, mentally, I picture them in the courtroom. People whose appearance works for and not against them definitely have the upper hand."

This doesn't mean you have to look like a movie star. But you do have to make a lasting first impression. Chapter 7, "Body English" should help you accomplish that goal.

Logistics also covers how you handle issues of time and place. An insurance underwriter with the now-defunct Kansas City branch of the New Hampshire Insurance Group ruefully remembers showing up late for an interview with another company in her office complex—because she got lost. When she found herself standing in the lobby of the wrong building with three minutes until interview time, she was visibly chagrined. Fortunately, the interviewer understood (and forgave), but such a gaffe can really throw your timing and self-control off.

When you do make mistakes like this, try to use them as rapport builders. Apologize, explain what happened (have a good reason) and move on. This will demonstrate your ability to handle mistakes honestly.

Paperwork presents another organizational issue. The night before interviews, pack your briefcase with extra copies of your resume, a notepad, pens, letters of recommendation and appropriate work samples. You don't want to be scrambling to throw everything together right before your meeting.

You'll also need a list of questions you want to ask. Design your questions so they (1) provide insight into which skills and experiences you should showcase and (2) provide information that will enable you to evaluate the job offer. In Chapter 9, "Your Turn to Ask," you'll find some ideas for formulating this strategy.

Good logistical organization means handling the issues of grooming, timing, transportation and presentation as effectively as possible. Most important, leave yourself enough time to prepare.

Negotiate

You should also be ready to talk money. To do so, you must have some idea what the industry pays for someone with your level of expertise. Professional associations often conduct salary surveys to provide members with this information. You also need to calculate your bottom line to make sure you don't sell yourself short.

But that doesn't mean you should automatically eliminate a position that *seems* too low. Your goal is to make the employer want you, *and then push for more money.*

To do that, you'll need to master some of the basic principles of salary negotiations. You'll find these outlined in Chapter 13: "Talking Money."

Practice Makes Perfect

"To be effective at interviewing, you need a practice-and-perfection mentality," says Bob Maher.

Mock interviews are a great way to get that experience. Team up with a job-hunting friend, or recruit your spouse into action. Have that person feed you some of the hard questions so you can practice your responses.

Videotaping your performance can really help, especially if you have a skilled interviewer at the other end of the mike. The strong visual impact of seeing yourself on tape can be more powerful than any objective feedback from a third party.

If you're just starting the interview process, doing some throwaway interviews will also help. Just as you wouldn't try out for the Olympics without any prior practice, your first interviews shouldn't be with your first-choice employers. Save those meetings for when you have your skills down pat.

Preparing and practicing offer both practical and emotional benefits.

"Preparation reduces the likelihood of lapses in form because it gives structure to the event," says Skip Sturman, director of Career Works, a Norwich, Vermont, career counseling firm.

Also, knowing what to expect (and feeling prepared to handle it) will familiarize you with the process and help reduce your anxiety.

Says Maher: "You have a much better chance of doing well in the interview when you feel like you're in your comfort zone."

But can you rehearse too much?

"People who are overprepared can sound wooden," says Sheryl Spanier, a senior consultant with Lee Hecht Harrison's New York office.

Or, says Maher, "too mechanical."

To be truly effective, you must strike a balance between the rehearsed response and the spontaneous impulse. Optimally, preparation should help you do that.

"The subtleties of perfection are real subtle," Maher says. "It's hard to get to the art if you don't have the skill."

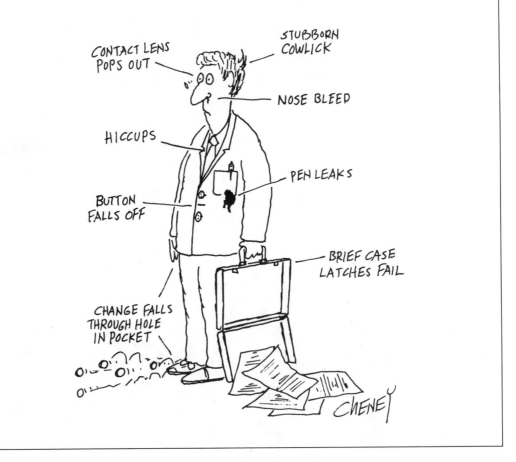

3

Typical
Questions

L egendary sportscaster and author Red Barber was once asked if deciding which questions to pose to which people was the toughest aspect of
being a professional interviewer. In his trademark Southern drawl, he
responded that coming up with questions was easy. Getting the folks
to provide meaningful answers was the hard part.

The same is true for company interviewers. That's why many rely on the
same nucleus of questions covering six areas of common concern regarding potential employees:

1. Suitability.

2. Employability.

3. Capability.

4. Compatibility.

5. Credibility.

6. Affordability.

The following sections review each concern.

Suitability

Before they waste too much precious time, employers want to know whether you're an appropriate candidate for the job. The most popular way to make that assessment usually involves some form of an icebreaker query, such as "Tell me about yourself." Since this request moves the candidate to center stage, it gives interviewers an opportunity to sit back and observe. For applicants who feel uncomfortable in the spotlight, this can be a particularly awkward moment. The key here is to decide on your strategy, rehearse it ad nauseum, then deliver your reply as though you were saying it for the first time.

"Tell me about yourself."

The experts agree: first and foremost, keep your answer short (1 to 2 minutes) but pithy. For example, career consultant Liz Branstead, in Pleaston, California, suggests the following formula:

My name is _____. I have _____ years of
experience as a _____. Recently, I worked for
_____ as a _____. Before that,
I worked for _____ as a _____.
My strengths are _____ (general) and _____ (technical).

"Memorize the formula and rehearse it," she says, "but make sure you take the time before each interview to change the words or focus to match the employer's values. For example, if they're antagonistic toward academia, it doesn't make sense to discuss your academic career."

There also should be a contextual component. After listing general areas of strengths, cite particular strengths (or, better yet, accomplishments) that position the information within a job context that fits the employer's marketplace; for example:

> I have more than 10 years of experience in the field of human resources development. Currently, I'm the director of human resources for _____, a retailer with more than 3,000 employees nationwide. My areas of expertise are labor relations, employee recruitment, training and development. You indicated that your organization is in the process of becoming unionized, and would like the HR director to help with that transition. Let me tell you about my experience at _____, where I represented management interests in that transition process . . .

The contextual component helps shift from a product-driven strategy to a market-driven approach. Here's another (market-driven) example:

> As you can see from my resume, I have more than 10 years of experience in sales and sales management. Most recently, I was the district sales manager for a major Chicago radio station. One of my strengths is in developing highly productive sales teams. For example, at _____, we doubled our revenues in a single year through innovative selling strategies and improved customer service. You indicated that you need someone in this position who can get results quickly. Having done that before, I'm confident that I can achieve that again for you.

Some counselors like to further enhance the rapport-building possibilities in the "tell me about yourself" statement by including some personal information.

FOR YOUR INFORMATION

TWO-MINUTE DRILL

Patricia Haskell, a career counselor in Bethesda, MD, suggests a two-minute drill that includes four 30-second quadrants: your early life and your education, followed by your work experience and your qualities/skills. She recommends scripting out quick sketches that discuss all four areas.

Jim Kacena, an outplacement consultant with Right Associates in Chicago, goes a step further by recommending that you present a 90-second commercial with three chronologically focused 30-second quadrants: (1) some personal information, (2) education and (3) a summary of experience.

Irene Mendelson, a career consultant in Bethesda, Maryland, says interviewees should start with personal information because "it helps develop a common ground." This approach has always felt comfortable to Mike Murphy, a former district sales manager with the Hoover Company in Wisconsin. Murphy begins his personal introduction with the statement "I'm married and my wife and I are expecting our first child." (He's since updated that intro to reflect his child's age.)

As long as the facts work for you, the use of personal information may help warm up the interview; but exercise good judgment. Former Caremark secretary Diana Kraus likes to lead with the fact that she was born and raised in Buffalo because it shows her long-term commitment to the community. She's less inclined, however, to mention that she's married and has four stepchildren, which might distract an interviewer too far from the primary focus of exploring job fit.

Candidates who have done their homework on the employer (and, therefore, know something about the organization's value system) might risk introducing personal information that seems compatible with those values. The key is to decide whether your personal information adds value to your candidacy. For example, companies whose mission includes a "commitment to the community" might welcome hearing more about your neighborhood involvement. Or, if you're aware that a company emphasizes strong family ties, you might mention your spouse and children in the conversation.

Offering personal data as a job-search technique has its detractors, though. Oak Park, Illinois, psychologist and career counselor Laurie Anderson thinks the whole "personal info" strategy is just too risky. "There are better ways to build rapport without inviting employers to judge your lifestyle choices." She recommends opening with a statement such as, "I'm excited to be here. I've heard a lot about your organization." If candidates want to use personal information, they should do so later in the interview, she says.

However much the experts disagree about the use of personal information, they unanimously agree that short is beautiful: First, it forces the interviewer to ask more questions and provide more direction; second, it prevents you from digressing into a long-winded chronology or life story that not only bores the interviewer to death but is largely beside the point.

One laid-off AT&T engineer in Chicago learned this lesson the hard way. Halfway through a blow-by-blow chronology of her work history, the interviewer interrupted and asked another question. As a result, the engineer never was able to discuss her most recent professional experience, which was the most sophisticated work she had done to date.

By offering the open-ended "tell me about yourself" query, "employers are most interested in hearing how candidates organize the information they present," says Joy Reed-Belt, president of an Oklahoma City outplacement and executive search firm. "People who wander all over the place don't make a very good impression."

She, too, isn't a big fan of giving personal information, but if you aren't sure how to proceed, she suggests asking interviewers what they really want to know. "Just don't overdo the technique by asking for a clarification of every question," she says.

Anderson also says that it's perfectly appropriate to ask employers to clarify the kind of information they're most interested in hearing. The only drawback is that it invites an interviewer to ask for more personal information than the candidate may be willing to give. (If you want to risk asking for direction, you'd better be prepared to take direction.)

Some employers take the initiative to redirect responses that aren't to their liking. A former Ameritech secretary remembers interviewing for a position with an employer who stopped her prepared commentary short with the response, "No. I want to hear about *you.*" To meet that demand, she then launched into a completely spontaneous discussion of her personal life, giving the employer a lot of information that would otherwise have been illegal to ask.

To handle this dilemma effectively, she should have set limits around the question by framing the discussion of her personal life in the context of the position. For example, she might say that she's married to an engineer who has been with _____ Company for _____ years (as a way of showing her stability and ties to the community). If her children are grown, she might say so because it means, ostensibly, that family crises won't pull her away from the job. If she has small children, she might introduce her (effective) solution to the child care issue along with the information. Or, she might choose to omit that information altogether (see Chapter 4 for ways to deal with illegal questions).

Decide on the strategy and information you want to include, but make sure you provide information that will really help you. For example, if you're a mother of three who thinks it's important for an employer to know that you'll sometimes have to leave work early, then you might take the risk of introducing that information (even though the employer may not like it). On the other hand, if the employer can't deal with that reality, then it's better you know now.

It's not only what you say, but how you say it that's important. Sheryl Spanier, a career consultant in New York, recalls one of her early interviews as a candidate. After she gave her prepared text, the interviewer responded: "Now that we've gotten that out of the way, tell me about you." He wasn't seeking personal information, but the spontaneous person behind the rehearsed response. From there, they went on to have a much more genuine conversation.

This is where Steven Sultanoff's "planned spontaneity" approach really pays off. Sultanoff, a psychologist in Newport Beach, California, says that candidates should prepare for tough interview situations by knowing how they want to respond, then deliver those responses in a totally spontaneous way. For Sultanoff, this often includes the use of humor, which helps the candidate come across as a real, three-dimensional person.

Other experts recommend closing out the response with a qualification question. Bob McCarthy likes to wind up his short commercial with a request for further instructions or direction such as "Does that answer your question?" or "Would you like me to elaborate on any particular experience?" This encourages interviewers to talk more about their needs and concerns.

Ideally, the goal of the "Tell me about yourself" statement is to establish rapport with the interviewer and lay the groundwork for a productive exploration of your mutual needs and goals.

Given that agenda, it can be very disconcerting to find yourself talking to an interviewer who is clearly distracted or disinterested.

An account executive who was interviewing for a position with an advertising agency remembers how unnerved she felt when she caught the interviewer staring out the window during her introductory statement.

Although it made her uncomfortable and self-conscious, she managed to plow through the rest of her recitation. But she couldn't help feeling that her speech had fallen on deaf ears.

What—if anything—could she have done differently?

Obviously, she needed a more interactive approach that would draw the interviewer back into the conversation. Although she would definitely want to resist the impulse to say "Am I boring you?", she could have politely asked "Would you like me to focus on something else?"

A computer programmer had a similar experience (albeit with a happier ending) while interviewing with a human resources representative. Halfway into his prepared statement, he noticed a glazed look in the interviewer's eyes and realized that she was no longer listening to him.

Flustered, he stopped mid-sentence and apologetically stammered "I'm afraid this isn't very interesting to you." To which, she replied "I'm not a techie. I feel like you're talking a foreign language."

Relieved, he adjusted his language to a more generalist audience and the rest of the interview proceeded more smoothly.

The task, of course, is to present relevant information in a language and style that will hold the employer's interest and promote discussion. In this latter example, the computer programmer wisely abandoned his prepared text to enter into a true conversation with the HR representative. And, in the process, he learned an important lesson about checking out an interviewer's response and making spontaneous adjustments to his script, when necessary.

Doug Richardson, a Philadelphia-based outplacement and career consultant, suggests a highly directed approach. He advises his clients to respond actively to the employer's most immediate needs and priorities. A typical Richardson response might sound like this:

> Probably the most relevant way to answer that question is in terms of the qualifications mentioned in your ad. As I understand it, you have an immediate need for someone who can increase your sales revenues through creative marketing strategies. Let me tell you about a time when I doubled my employer's sales revenues through a unique direct mail marketing campaign.

But what if you don't have enough information about the organization or its needs to build an immediate match? Simple, Richardson says. Ask for more information:

> I'd like to tell you about myself, Ms. Employer, but I think the most relevant way to do that is in terms of your position needs. So, if you can tell me a little more about the position, I can better address your question.

With this strategy, you ask simultaneously for a qualification of the question and set limits to the inquiry.

This highly goal-oriented strategy enables an interviewee to really seize control of the situation and direct the outcome of the conversation. But it takes a certain personality style to carry it off effectively.

Many candidates don't feel entirely comfortable with this level of self-assertion. They prefer to ease into the conversation with more of a building-block approach.

Patricia Berg, an outplacement executive in Bloomington, Minnesota, suggests that candidates start with an overview or historical perspective highlighting skills that seem most relevant to the employer's needs. They should anchor that information with a story about a specific accomplishment, then "pass the baton" back to the interviewer by saying, "Now that I've told you about myself, can you tell me a little more about the position?"

My personal favorite is a process-oriented strategy that also anticipates and answers several typical questions at once. Like many experts, I recommend starting with a brief summary or overview, highlighting major areas of experience and education (I'm not a big fan of personal info, either). Basically, this is an overview of past accomplishments—a short history of who you are to date.

Next, move more directly into the immediate present with an explanation of why you're looking for work (I need a more challenging position; my job at _____ was eliminated, etc.). Knowing that employers inevitably ask this question, candidates who introduce this information early on avoid some of the "automatic pilot" part of interviews and move faster to more important things.

Then mention how you heard about the position and why you're interested in it. It draws the interviewer out of the observer role and into greater participation. Once you have the person's undivided attention (because you're talking about something the employer really cares about), present a more focused view of your specific qualifications for the position. Anchor that information with a story about a time when you accomplished something similar to what the employer seems to want. Finally, use the "Berg close" ("Now that I've told you about myself, can you tell me more about the position?") because it addresses another main objective of the interview: a mutual exploration of job fit.

The potential downside to my strategy? It might take three to four minutes, and that can feel like a long time to people who really feel self-conscious when talking about themselves.

Employability

Employers are generally a cautious lot. Bad hires are risky business. They want a guarantee, if possible, that they're buying a solution to their problems, not more trouble. To reassure themselves of a candidate's employability, they inevitably want to know, "Why are you leaving (or did you leave) your present employer?" In your response, they'll be looking for signs of instability, performance problems or culpability.

Why did you leave (are leaving) your last job?

Situation 1: You got fired

This particular question is hardest on people who have been fired, so let's deal with this candidate group up front.

First of all, recognize that getting fired usually is a traumatic experience that generates lots of negative emotions. You need to process this event (both emotionally and, if possible, objectively) so you can give an emotionally neutral response. Otherwise, it won't matter what you say; you'll give yourself away with how you say it.

Pat Berg argues for "perspective." "Remember, this is an event in your career. It's not your whole career. People survive the experience."

In fact, "the good news is that lots of people go on to better situations," says Bob McCarthy.

The key is in your attitude.

Marianne Ruggiero, a corporate senior vice president in New York, says she prefers candidates who admit they got fired. "But I also want to hear them tell me what lesson they learned from their mistake so I know it won't be repeated if they come to work for us." Like many employers, Ruggiero realizes that mistakes happen. The important thing, she says, is how people deal with the circumstances.

A lot of this is simply a matter of practice. It's a question of finding the right way to explain the circumstances without becoming critical or self-defensive. Humor is one ideal way to handle the situation. As one McCarthy protégé said, "The ax has been very, very good to me."

Mostly, employers need reassurance that you are OK, so find a way to give it to them. There is beauty here in brevity. It's a good idea to keep your answer short and emotionally positive (or, at least neutral). This may or may not include the actual statement, "I got fired," but if it does, always include some lesson learned; an understanding that will, in some way, benefit future employers.

"When someone gets fired because of a personality conflict, it usually makes sense to talk in terms of a 'mismatch' or 'bad fit,'" Anderson says. "That keeps the element of blame out of the picture."

In its most abbreviated form, this involves a simple, "It didn't work out." Employers who want to know can probe more deeply, but the interviewee always has the right to set limits on the inquiry. The key here is to assuage employer concerns without becoming defensive or resentful. For some, this means coming up with a well-rehearsed explanation.

An account executive with a temporary personnel agency in Chicago was fired when her co-workers banded together and complained to her supervisor about her attitude. Despite a solid sales record of achievements, the woman lost her job because her presence was simply too disruptive to the rest of the office. After some practice (which included some emotional catharsis), she was able to deliver the following bias-free explanation:

Although my sales figures were good (I managed to bring in 50 new accounts in the first year of operation), there wasn't a good personality match. Although I can usually fit in very well, in this office everyone was at least 20 years younger than me. Unfortunately, they came to their decision sooner than I did. But it taught me an important lesson about myself. I need a professional environment with a mixed group of people. Can you tell me a little more about your organization?

This particular response has several key features that "firees" may want to adopt. First, it acknowledges the existence of a problem without placing blame. Nevertheless, the candidate manages to say (or imply) several positive things about herself: First, her performance—as evidenced by her sales accomplishments—was good; second, the mismatch occurred because of her strengths (maturity and professionalism) rather than a weakness. She also emphasizes that she learned an important lesson from the experience with regard to what she wants and needs from an organization. Then, she proves her point by asking the interviewer to provide more information about the organization.

If you've been fired for personality conflicts, offer to produce references at this point to reassure employers that this was an isolated incident that is unlikely to recur.

Situation 2: You got laid off

Once upon a time, people expected to keep their jobs for life. No more. The massive restructuring of the workplace has made job security a remnant of the past. As a result, many otherwise stable employees are now pounding the pavement for new jobs.

The good news is that the stigma of unemployment is mostly gone, especially when performance issues aren't a factor. For these folks, the experts recommend that candidates keep it short, neutral and closely tied to the big picture by saying "My job was phased out," "My division moved to Atlanta" or "My company was sold." In other words, it wasn't personal and you aren't taking it personally.

Poor performers do get washed out during reorganizations. For those whose last performance reviews looked less than stellar, it might be helpful to know that employers cannot, by law, say anything that would prohibit you from getting another job. When called for references, most companies steer clear of potential legal liabilities by indicating only the dates you worked there, your job title and a verification of your salary. Given these circumstances, it usually makes sense to tie the reasons for the layoff to the organizational restructuring without introducing the performance issue.

Another word of caution. People who get laid off often have many conflicting feelings about the experience. New employers may be reluctant to hire people who are carrying that kind of emotional baggage because those folks aren't psychologically ready to give their all to a new position. These people need to do some "emotional homework" first (see Chapter 6). Otherwise, those feelings will undoubtedly spill out in the interview.

Situation 3: There's no room for advancement or growth

Another group of job changers move because they feel stuck. They jump ship to get ahead or develop new skills and experiences. For them, the response to the "Why are you leaving" question should revolve around the skills and experiences they hope to use and develop with a new employer. To customize this to the specific interview, focus on those developmental areas that are most important to you. Then, use a probing question to explore the reality of what the employer has to offer.

One software trainer chose to emphasize her need for a different, "more hands-on" manager. Although she described herself as a self-motivated worker, she felt she could learn from someone who was more involved with the staff. Then she threw the ball back into the interviewer's court by asking, "Can you tell me a little more about your management style?"

Since her job wasn't in jeopardy and she could afford to wait until she found the right position, this proved to be an absolutely no-risk strategy.

Describe a time when you failed. Employers want to know that people are capable of learning from their mistakes. Says Ruggiero: "I look for a learning attitude, because people who have stopped learning are dangerous. My bias is toward people who can learn from mistakes. I don't care if you failed, but I do want to know why."

For Ruggiero, how people handle failure is a good test of character. "People who learn from failure usually have courage and discipline." Joy Reed-Belt agrees: "When people have learned from their mistakes, they don't repeat them. I look for someone who can own their mistakes and grow from them."

Capability

"A significant shift has taken place in the past 10 years," says Marianne Ruggiero. "Because of all the downsizings, employers need people who can really pull their weight and add value to the organization." Toward that objective, employers ask candidates lots of questions about their skills and experience. These questions assume that past behavior is the best predictor of future performance.

What are your strengths?

By this, an employer means "What do you do best?" Savvy interviewees would do well to answer this question in terms of the specific job requirements. For example, for a position that requires good "platform" skills, make sure to include such skills as one of your strengths. If your answer, however, is little more than a string of nouns and adjectives, it probably won't clinch the deal.

Says Laurie Anderson: "It isn't enough to speak in vague generalities. You have to back up your assertions with behavioral evidence that's concrete and compelling." You might say:

> My strongest abilities are organizational, problem-solving and interpersonal communication. Let me tell you about a project that required all three . . .

Anderson says that the coherency of the statement is really important because it shapes the employer's understanding of your abilities. While it isn't necessary to integrate all your strengths into a cohesive whole, you do need to tie each strength into your understanding of the employer's needs. Translate the question into "What can you do for me?"

Again, there is a good argument for homework—know as much about an employer's needs and concerns (before the interview) as possible. When that information isn't available (or there isn't time to do the research), candidates have two choices:

☆ Press for some facts from the interviewer: Mr. Employer, I'd be happy to tell you about my strengths, but it would help if I knew more about the position so that I could focus on those strengths that will be most helpful to you. (In other words, I have so much to offer, I don't know where to begin.)

☆ Focus on selling general "liberal arts" type skills, such as project management, problem solving or being a team player, attributes that most
companies will undoubtedly value.

"But don't just go through a litany of buzzwords," says Jim Kacena. "The example
is what makes it meaningful. The buzzword by itself is useless since employers
have already heard it all."

Diana Kraus has developed a cohesive response to the "What are your
strengths?" question by identifying (and then illustrating) three key attributes:

1. "I get things done—no matter what it takes." To illustrate her point,
   Kraus tells a story of a time when her boss at Goldome Bank in Buffalo
   wanted to celebrate the introduction of a new product with a real bull to
   symbolize a "bull market." She then describes some of the logistics involved in actually bringing a bull to a sales promotion.

2. "I thrive on crisis." To illustrate that working style, she tells the story of a
   time when Goldome was taken over by the FDIC. The takeover created
   mass panic among the pensioners who were concerned that their benefits
   would be cut off. Amid the pandemonium, it was Kraus's job to calm people down, track down the information they needed and do what was necessary to restore their peace of mind.

3. "I'm a hard worker, so I really like working for hard-driving executives."
   From there, Kraus describes a highly successful working relationship
   with her former boss, citing specific details about how they formed a successful partnership that really got things done.

By using these three examples, Kraus is able to create a consistent (and impressive) picture of herself as a highly motivated, cooperative and adaptable employee
who thrives on challenge, pressure and responsibility. Who wouldn't want to hire
that profile?

What are your weaknesses?

Nobody ever seems to ask about your strengths without also asking about your
weaknesses. Although it may seem like a stupid question, it's amazing how many
candidates knock themselves out of the competition with their responses.

Preparation is vital. By deciding in advance how you want to answer this question, you should never be caught unprepared (at least, not if you stick to the game plan). Here are your choices:

Strategy 1: Present a weakness that's really a hidden strength

Let me give you a personal example. Some of my colleagues like to refer to me as a "warm and fuzzy counselor." By that, they mean that they find me warm, sensitive and compassionate. In certain situations, having such a empathic style can make my job more painful—and therefore tougher. (I cried the first time I had to fire someone.) But in most of the counseling settings, where I work, that style has proved more of an asset than a liability. Translated into the language of "weaknesses," I might say, "Some people find my counseling style too soft. But my clients usually appreciate my heart."

A potential drawback of the "strength as weakness" strategy is that it can appear phony and self-serving. Such commonly used statements as "I'm a perfectionist" or "I'm a workaholic" are too transparent to be effective.

Strategy 2: Cite a corrected weakness

Another weakness strategy is to cite something that you are working to correct. For example, "In my current position, I haven't had the opportunity to do much "C" programming. So I'm taking a course at the university to get my skills up to speed. (This assumes you aren't applying for a job as a "C" programmer.)

Strategy 3: Cite a lesson learned

Similar to the "corrected weakness" strategy, this approach uses a "lesson-learned" story. Says Joy Reed-Belt, an Oklahoma City career consultant and author: "I don't want to hear someone say, 'I never made a mistake' because I know they aren't telling the truth. If I'm interviewing a lender, for example, I don't want to hear 'I never made a bad loan.' I want to hear them say what lengths they went to in order to collect the bad loan, and what safeguards they've since put in place. Then I know they learned a lesson that isn't likely to be repeated."

In this strategy, focus on a specific mistake rather than a generalized area of weakness. And "never tell a weakness without telling about the recovery," says Reed-Belt.

Strategy 4: Cite a lapsed skill (that you prefer not to use again)

This strategy involves choosing a skill area unrelated to the responsibilities of the job. Example: Since moving into a management position, my clerical skills have really gotten rusty. (**Message:** Don't push me back down the ladder.)

Strategy 5: Cite an unrelated skill

"I really need to work on my French" (assuming the job does not require French language skills).

Strategy 6: Cite a learning objective

"I would really like to get more exposure to the international market." This strategy has an added value: It sets you up perfectly to say, "Can you tell me more about your plans in the international arena?"

Strategy 7: Try humor

One of my favorite stories comes from a former sales manager who loved to say, "Ask my parole officer." Other witty responses to the query "What are your weaknesses" might be "Second serves," "golf putts" and "chocolate ice cream." If you use the humorous approach, however, you must follow up with a real answer. Otherwise, the interviewer will feel that you're being too manipulative and evasive.

Strategy 8: Reaffirm your qualifications

"Nothing that affects my ability to do this job." (If the employer presses you for something more specific, name something unrelated. It will prove your first point.)

The key here is to never name anything that will really hurt you. "I can't get along with people," "I hate paperwork" or "I can't get out of bed in the morning" make bad interview sense. As did one candidate's candid remark: "I usually nod off at about 3:00 o'clock every day."

Preparation for the "weakness" question is imperative because it replaces the spontaneous response with a well-rehearsed answer. And when your weaknesses are the focal point of a discussion, it's best not to be too spontaneous.

Occasionally, an employer will ask for more than one weakness. When that happened to Jerry Hannigan, he went back to the drawing board to see if he could come up with two more deficiencies. A better response? "Offhand, I can't think of three weaknesses. But I can tell you one that I have been working really hard to correct . . ."

If you could do anything in your career differently, what would it be?

As interviewees have become more sophisticated in their ability to handle the "weakness" question, employers have started to look for new ways to unearth vulnerabilities. In many cases, this strategy has worked effectively.

Take, for example, one of my highly experienced colleagues who blurted out, "I should have gone to Vassar." Until that moment, her education had never been considered a liability. But her response tipped the employer off to some unresolved conflict.

In another case, a secretary was prone to say, "If I had it all to do over again, I think I'd choose a different career." Since she was still looking for a secretarial job, it probably wasn't the best time to show her ambivalence about her career choice. After hearing her own spontaneous response, this woman decided on a different strategy. "Now, I tell employers that there wasn't enough growth in my first secretarial job. I really need and enjoy a challenge, which is what I'm hoping to get from them."

The rules here are the same. Don't mention anything major. Don't introduce liabilities that don't show. And, whenever possible, invite the employer to offer a remedy to that particular dissatisfaction.

What is your greatest achievement?

Customize, customize, customize. Choose an example that best illustrates your capability for this specific job. If I were interviewing for a position that required new business development, I would undoubtedly highlight the marketing and public relations strategies I've used to build my private counseling practice. As a capstone, I might even produce (or offer to produce) a copy of a full-page interview with me that appeared in the *Chicago Sunday Tribune Magazine,* with the comment that it generated more than 100 new clients.

My examples might change depending on the employer's intended market. For example, if they were interested in pursuing government contracts, I might mention that I had been the regional career counselor for the Nuclear Regulatory Commission for five years.

If professionals were the intended market, I might mention my participation as a speaker at several American Medical Association, American Bar Association and Chicago Bar Association events. On the other hand, if I were interviewing for a position with a psychiatric hospital, I would be more inclined to discuss my case consultations with Northwestern Memorial Hospital and the University of Chicago hospital staff.

What you choose to view as your "best" accomplishment is largely situational. Rather than falling into the trap of conveying an unrelated accomplishment, focus your answer (as closely as possible) on your understanding of the employer's needs.

Unfortunately, words like "best," "worst" and "failure" invite excess emotionalism. Don't let the interviewer goad you into an inappropriate response with these measures. Show your true colors by speaking to both sides of the issue with clarity.

Compatibility

It's not enough to have the proper skill set. Employers also want to know if (and how) you'll fit into their organization. Toward that end, they tend to ask many "relationship" questions, particularly regarding your attitude toward authority and co-workers.

What would your former boss say about you?

Body language is often a big tip-off here. People with negative experiences tend to look and act defensively. Long before the question is answered, the interviewer knows there was "trouble in paradise."

If there was a problem, try to neutralize it by focusing your answer on the productive parts of the relationship: "We were able to work together to accomplish shared goals. For example, let me tell you about the time . . . ," or "We didn't always agree; but we were always able to work out our differences."

If there were stylistic differences, try to paint them in neutral terms, Anderson suggests. "Then, look for the task-related issues that didn't interfere with getting the job done."

There are times when the relationship really has been disastrous. In these instances, it's important to take some ownership for your particular style. Rather than bad-mouthing former supervisors, talk in terms of the kind of reporting relationship that works best for you.

Says Diana Kraus, "I really need a lot of freedom and responsibility. I can't have someone looking over my shoulder every minute."

There's some risk in stating your needs: The employer may not have what you want. If that's the case, though, it's better to know that up front and keep looking, says counselor Irene Mendelson, "because you won't be happy there, anyway."

As long as you got along well with your boss, you could probably just speak naturally. Words that come to mind should be fun, challenging, exciting and productive. But if you feel more conflicted, take time to reflect on some of the positive things you accomplished together, then showcase those.

How do you handle authority?

This is a more generalized version of the previous question, but gives you more leeway to select your best experiences with bosses. From there, it's a short step to talking about how (and with whom) you work best.

What would your colleagues say about you?

Treat this question similarly to the authority questions. Focus on the productive aspects of your relationships, and anchor your response with a story. Then discuss your preferred team role. As team play becomes an increasingly important employment concern, expect recruiters to try to learn more about your community needs. Welcome their curiosity because it opens the door for you to learn more about the type of company culture they can offer.

While "style questions" are an important component of the compatibility quotient, your career goals can be an asset or liability as well.

Where do you want to be five years from now?

The experts agree: It isn't a good idea to express position objectives. "It's the 'kiss of death' to say 'I'd like to have your job,' because maybe the person is planning to keep that job awhile longer," says Jim Kacena.

Management consultant Richard Silverman agrees: "Show an interest in the current job and in making a contribution to the organization." And Laurie Anderson adds that you should talk about the levels of responsibility you'd like to attain, and that your primary goal is to add value to the organization. "Show ambition," she says, "but don't commit to a specific job title."

This strategy worked well for one financial sales rep in Chicago who was able to articulate three possible career directions: international sales, sales management and marketing. By expressing this kind of latitude and flexibility, he opened the door to a discussion of the employer's plans and goals, and was pleased to discover that two of his three career objectives (international sales and sales management) were indeed feasible. This, in turn, led to a fruitful discussion of the company's plan to penetrate the global marketplace, as well as its attitude toward promoting candidates out of the sales ranks. When the offer arrived, he jumped to accept.

Although many interviewees are reluctant to lay their cards on the table quite so plainly, it really does help to know whether you and your future employer have mutually compatible goals. Otherwise, it may be a very unhappy employment partnership.

Bob McCarthy likens the idea of risk taking to the metaphor of the turtle, a reptile that has managed to survive hundreds of thousands of years by sticking its neck out in order to move. "You have to be brave," McCarthy says. "Identify the risk you're willing to take, then take it." Sometimes that risk involves saying what you want and need to make your contribution count.

Credibility

Some people will say (or do) anything to get a job—even lie. Knowing this, employers often make it a practice to ask for (and check) references.

Can we check your references?

Employers are doublechecking here for reservations. If you have none, there's no better time for a spontaneous, "Of course!" Naturally, it helps if you've cleared the path to that spontaneous response by knowing which references you want to use (and what they're going to say about you).

One (now retired) district sales manager made that abundantly clear when one of his subordinates used his name as a reference without consulting him. "Even though I knew it was technically wrong," the former manager says, "I felt that I needed to be honest. So I said 'He's a helluva good employee, but sometimes he has a drinking problem.'" Although he later advised his employee not to use him as a reference again, in the meantime, the damage was done.

Irene Mendelson encourages her clients to call their references ahead of time to discuss the available position. When your references know the type of job you're hoping to fill, they can offer information that strengthens your candidacy by highlighting your most relevant skills. "A lukewarm reference will hurt you almost as much as a negative one," says Mendelson.

If you're on good terms with your references (if you aren't, you shouldn't be using them), they won't object to a little "prepping." In fact, most will welcome the assistance.

There are times when your answer to the reference question must be no, but with an explanation. If you'd like to keep your job search confidential, you obviously won't want interviewers contacting your present employer. However, if you have former bosses, co-workers or even clients who can vouch for your performance, this will assure interviewers that you have nothing to hide.

If your former employer won't give you a good reference, you might want to try a "yes, but" strategy. Since past employers cannot, by law, say anything that would prohibit you from getting another job, you can say, "You're welcome to contact my former employer, but it's their policy not to give references."

Affordability

Employers and candidates alike often are anxious about the question of money. Nobody wants to waste time and energy wanting what they can't afford to buy. But, in fact, until both parties know more about each other, there really isn't anything to talk about. Therefore, the first order of business should be jointly figuring out whether you want to work together. Sometimes, however, employers try to "jump the gun" by prematurely asking money questions.

How much money are you looking for?

Unless the employer is prepared to make you a job offer, ask politely to defer salary discussions until it's clear that a partnership is desirable. One way to do this is by saying, "I'm sure when the time comes, we'll be able to work out a fair compensation package. For now, if you don't mind, I prefer to focus on whether we really have a match here."

Says Jim Kacena: "Don't talk money until you have a job offer. Period. Because until you have an offer, you don't have any negotiating power."

Another way of responding to the question is to state honestly that, until you know more about the position and the organization, you really aren't prepared to make a salary demand. Therefore, your time would probably be better spent discussing the employment opportunity. In this statement, you convey that you expect to be paid to do a certain job, but that until you know more about what that job is, there's no way to know what your salary requirements will be.

If an employer pushes for a dollar figure (or refuses to proceed unless you answer the question), be prepared to back down a little from this primary strategy. Never risk alienating the interviewer. However, don't lock yourself into any specific numbers. Instead, do some advance research on salary levels for similar positions within the same industry (and company size, if possible). Professional associations are a great place to find this information; you also can review the weekly salary surveys published in the *National Business Employment Weekly*. Then, tell the employer that based on your understanding of the market value for the position, you would expect your compensation to be in the range of $_____.

Under no circumstances, however, should you allow yourself to be drawn into premature negotiations. Until you have an offer, the less said the better. If you aren't sure whether the employer is actually making you an offer (or preparing to make an offer), ask directly, "Are you making me an offer?" If the answer is in the affirmative, then be prepared to negotiate. Otherwise, hold off until the timing is right. (Chapter 13 covers the entire process of salary negotiations.)

How much are you presently earning?

Some experts recommend that you treat this question as if the employer had asked, "How much money are you looking for?" Then follow the same procedures for deferring the discussion until you have a job offer.

Again, if the employer seems antagonized by the evasion, hedge your bets with a response such as, "I can tell you how much I was earning in my previous position, but until I know more about the responsibility of this particular job, I can't really tell you how much money I'm looking for."

In this way, you can separate current earnings from future negotiations, a strategy that's particularly effective if you're seeking a higher-paying position.

One final note: If you choose to reveal your current earnings, talk in ballpark figures rather than exact numbers. This will leave you some leeway for future negotiations.

Suggestions for All Interview Situations

In general, your strategy when responding to typical interview questions should be to listen carefully and answer only what was asked. Then probe for how the employer felt about your response and, if necessary, elaborate. Finally, seize the opportunity to ask a related question in return that will help you determine whether the position offers a truly good employment match.

Always try to be as positive as possible. If it isn't possible to be positive, strive for emotional neutrality. Don't let some of the negative phraseology employers like to use deter you from the main event of selling yourself and learning more about the position. However, a preponderance of negative questions may tell you something important about the employer that can't be ignored. Since you should expect all people to treat you with respect, don't allow a job interviewer to be the exception.

Finally, although experts all argue strongly for the value of preparation—which obviously includes developing and rehearsing your responses to many of the typical questions employers expect to ask—no one believes that interviewees should turn themselves into parrots.

Try to maintain the integrity of the interview situation by responding as one human being to another. While this may not guarantee that you'll finesse every interview and, therefore, get every offer, you'll feel better about your involvement in the process. Ultimately, you'll find a better job match if you manage your side of the task with common sense and honesty.

COMMONLY ASKED QUESTIONS

Many other standard or "typical" questions may arise during interviews. Look over the following list and develop a response for each question. Use the space given to complete your answers, or make a photocopy of these pages to use as a worksheet before each interview.

Have you done the best work you are capable of?

_____

_____

What have you learned from each of your jobs?

_____

_____

Which of your jobs was the least interesting? Why?

_____

_____

Which job did you like the most?

_____

_____

What kind of an employee are you?

_____

_____

Describe your personality.

_____

_____

On your last performance evaluation, what did your supervisor criticize you for?

_____

_____

How do you normally handle criticism? Give an example.

_____

_____

Describe a situation when you feel you were unfairly criticized. What did you do?

_____

_____

What are your weaknesses?

_____

_____

What have you done to correct those weaknesses?

_____

_____

Have you ever failed?

_____

_____

How do you normally handle failure?

_____

_____

What did you like most about your last job?

_____

_____

What did you dislike the most about your last job?

_____

_____

What are you looking for in your next job?

_____

_____

Have you ever been fired or asked to resign? Why?

_____

_____

Why have you held so many jobs?

_____

_____

Why did you stay with one company so long?

_____

_____

Do you consider yourself a loyal employee?

_____

_____

What are your career goals/objectives?

_____

_____

How does this job fit in with your career goals?

_____

_____

How do you feel about further training?

_____

_____

How do you normally handle change?

_____

_____

Would you like to have your boss's job?

_____

_____

Why haven't you progressed more in your career?

_____

_____

Do you consider yourself a success?

_____

_____

Have you ever been turned down for a raise?

_____

_____

Why aren't you earning more money at your age?

_____

_____

Do you consider yourself promotable?

_____

_____

What is the hardest thing you ever had to do in your job?

_____

_____

How would you describe your boss's style?

_____

_____

How would your boss describe your style?

_____

_____

How would you describe your relationship with your boss?

_____

_____

What have you learned from your boss?

_____

_____

When you are supervising people, how do you motivate them?

_____

_____

Describe a time when you resolved a conflict between two of your subordinates.

_____

_____

What would your subordinates say about you?

_____

_____

What do you look for in an employee?

_____

_____

How do you normally relate to "office politics"?

_____

_____

Describe a time when you got caught up in office politics unfairly.

_____

_____

Do you prefer to work alone or with others?

_____

_____

Do you consider yourself a team player?

_____

_____

Describe your style as a team player.

_____

_____

Do you consider yourself self-motivated? Describe a time when you took the initiative to accomplish something.

_____

_____

Name three personal characteristics that best describe you.

_____

_____

What motivates you?

_____

_____

Describe your relationship with peers.

_____

_____

How do you handle conflict with peers?

_____

_____

What kind of people do you prefer to work with?

_____

_____

What kind of people do you dislike the most?

_____

_____

What were the people like at your last company?

_____

_____

What did you like least about your last employer?

_____

_____

What did you like the most about your last employer?

_____

_____

If you could change one thing about your last employer, what would it be?

_____

_____

Were you satisfied with your performance at your last company?

_____

_____

Were they satisfied with you?

_____

_____

Tell me about a time when you failed personally.

_____

_____

How do you handle failures or weaknesses in others?

_____

_____

How would you describe your attitude toward risk?

_____

_____

Do you consider yourself a risk taker?

_____

_____

How do you normally handle crises?

_____

_____

Tell me about a time when you were under a great deal of pressure.

_____

_____

What kind of decisions are most difficult for you?

_____

_____

Why has it taken you so long to find a new job?

_____

_____

Why does this job interest you?

_____

_____

How is this job different from the other positions you have interviewed for?

_____

_____

What kind of contribution do you think you could make to our organization?

_____

_____

What part of this job interests you the most?

_____

_____

What part of this job interests you the least?

_____

_____

How long do you plan to stay?

_____

_____

What makes you different from other candidates?

_____

_____

Where else are you interviewing?

_____

_____

When are you available to start?

_____

_____

Is there anything that I have forgotten to ask you?

_____

_____

"Of course, there will be other duties as directed."

4

Red Flags

D o you want to do this job?" "Do you have the right skills?" "Will you fit in?"

Sometimes employers try to pry into your history or peer into your psyche in ways that feel emotionally dangerous or offensive. However, you don't have to be a happy victim to the inquisition. You just have to know how to set limits or boundaries around the inquiry.

Learning to handle employers' sometimes less-than-tactful probings may take some practice (and a bit of a thick skin). The process begins with understanding your personal areas of vulnerability. Perhaps you feel you're too old (or that others will feel that you're too old). You're sensitive to sexism, racism, or religious discrimination. You got booted out of your last job and are sure that no one will ever hire you again. Or, you didn't get booted out—but you secretly suspect you deserved to be. You're worried that references will sabotage your job search and ruin your future.

The interview process can be a learning experience, so pay attention to tough questions or sensitive issues that employers seem to bring up repeatedly. Then work on finding ways to neutralize those objections with convincing responses. At the same time, realize that tough questions often are more a matter of perception than reality.

When Patrice Becicka, a former tax supervisor in Cedar Rapids, Iowa, interviewed for a compliance position with a local manufacturer, she was asked a host of questions about her work relationships: How did you get along with your supervisor? What did you like most about him or her? What did you like least? What did you learn from your boss? What was your relationship with subordinates like? What did they like most about you? What did they like least about you?

For people who have a history of conflict with bosses and co-workers, this can feel more like a third-degree grilling than a job interview, but Becicka didn't see it that way. Because she loved her job, got along well with and learned a lot from her supervisor, and always managed a productive team of employees, she warmed considerably to the challenge presented by this line of questioning.

In general, when your experiences are good you have less to defend so you can trust your spontaneous responses. Not so for those experiences which are painful—especially if they remain unresolved.

Phyllis Ravin is much less enthusiastic about interviewing. When Ravin decided to sell her insurance business and start job hunting, she never dreamed how difficult it would be to find regular working hours and a steady paycheck with benefits. She's only in her 40s but some employers question whether she can fit in with much younger co-workers. Others fear she's overqualified: that she'll get bored and leave as soon as something better comes along. Then, there are the employers who are sticklers for the college degree she doesn't have. To them, she's more under- than overqualified. Plus, she's been asked by five different employers to complete the same personality assessment exercise. She hasn't received any feedback (or an offer). On the fifth go-round, she refused to take the exercise again.

She's caught in a Catch-22. The more objections she encounters, the more angry and frustrated she becomes; and the angrier and more frustrated she becomes, the more objections she encounters.

To break that cycle, Ravin needs a more effective strategy for handling objections. Like many interviewees, she seems to view an objection as a rejection (or at least the precursor to one) and gets defensive.

Says Tom Washington: "An objection isn't a rejection. It's simply a request for more information. It means that the interviewer isn't yet completely sold on you."

Good interviewees get more control during interviews by learning to handle "no sale" signals when they surface. Like the salesperson who learns to "embrace the no" (because it gets the transaction closer to 'yes'), interviewees can learn to appreciate the golden opportunity to melt down an interviewer's objection with an effective response.

Employment History

Because past history often predicts future performance, employers are (understandably) concerned when work histories include too much job-hopping, employment gaps or unexplained terminations. Savvy interviewees can gain employers' confidence and trust by reassuring them that they have no such liabilities.

Job-Hopping

Says Ed Goedert, president of an Oakbrook, Illinois, psychological testing firm:

> When a corporation hires me to assess a candidate's suitability for a certain position, I always look at their career moves. I want to know why they changed jobs and where they think they're headed so I can determine if they'll be happy in the position that's available.

If you don't know where you're headed (or do know—but took a long time to find out), it's easy to get defensive about your career history. But it won't help your cause. You're better off trying to lead with whatever positives were gleaned from the experience.

After 15 productive years in the real-estate industry, a client of mine lost his job when his firm closed up shop. Because his industry was going through a massive crisis, his next three jobs were very short-lived: In each case, the firms went belly-up.

He decided to change careers but had trouble finding anything he liked (or that paid) half as much. For the next four years, he wandered through the job market like a shell-shocked war victim—taking and discarding a series of entry-level jobs.

By the time he decided to settle into the field of public relations, he had a whole lot of explaining to do to future employers—most of whom were worried that he was unstable. In fact, he wanted desperately to find a place where he could settle down and stay. "If I never look for another job again," he says, "it will be too soon for me."

It's crucial that this candidate plan exactly how to approach the job-hopping issue so he can relax in interviews, instead of waiting nervously for employers to drop the bombshell question.

Rather than elaborate on the years of angst he experienced after being stripped of his professional identity, he decided simply to share his (hard-earned) resolution of the problem and keep the gory details to himself. The answer we composed is short and to the point:

> I was really committed to my career in real estate. Once that was no longer possible, it took me awhile to figure out what I wanted to do. But, in the meantime, I had to pay the bills.
> Through my volunteer work at _____,
> I discovered that I really love public relations. I think my skills translate particularly well to the corporate communications position available here, which is what I'm here to pursue with you. . . .

FOR YOUR INFORMATION

DEFUSE LOADED QUESTIONS

Carol Hyatt and Linda Gottlieb, authors of *Why Smart People Fail,* suggest a four-step procedure for developing emotionally neutral responses to dangerous questions:

1. Write down a brief statement of the event (e.g., "I lost my job").
2. Tell your side of the story.
3. Review it for negative, self-defeating assumptions.
4. Reinterpret the event in a more positive way.

This response is good because it doesn't apologize or overexplain, yet it's honest and reassuring. He sounds like someone who's resolved his negative feelings and is ready to get on with his career. By putting the best face on the truth, he'll have a better chance of accomplishing that goal.

It can take some practice to get your spiel down pat, as the following story demonstrates.

Seven years ago, "Sandy" graduated from the University of Missouri with a BS in journalism and got her first job as a cub reporter on a small-town newspaper. Not cut out for small-town life, she quit her job after 18 months and moved back home where she worked as a hostess in her family's restaurant business while pursuing another writing job. It took her almost a year to land a position with a local cable television channel, where she was involved in the writing, producing and on-air delivery of a weekly news show.

She loved the work, but the pay was abysmal. Seven months later, she jumped ship for a better-paying media relations position with a health care association. She stayed there for 3½ years. Then, when her husband was transferred to a new city, she quit her job to move with him.

Viewed from one perspective, Sandy's job changes have always been governed more by life needs—small-town blues, financial concerns, marital harmony—than career development. Any employer reviewing her career history might naturally wonder, when her personal needs will next interrupt her employment situation. Knowing this, Sandy deemphasizes many of the personal lifestyle issues that motivated her decisions in the past. Her scenario sounds something like this:

> I view the early years of my career as a period of experimentation. Mostly, I was figuring out who I am professionally and what I'm really good at—which is media communications. Now that I have a broad range of experiences, I'm ready to put them together in one position that will utilize my strengths in writing and presenting information to (or for) the media.

By stressing her career-development goals, she presents herself as an ambitious self-directed careerist who knows who she is and what she wants.

Employment Gaps

Employment gaps provide another potential red flag to employers. While many career paths are no longer a single upward trajectory, it still matters what you did with your time out. Employers aren't really all that interested in your personal life, they just want to make sure that you're ready, willing and able to commit to a job with them.

Linda Bougie, a career consultant with CareerLabs Ltd. in Englewood, Colorado, recommends telling employers how you grew professionally during breaks in employment. "Regardless of whether it was volunteer work, parenthood or job hunting that kept you busy, there's always something you can learn from the experience," she says.

Even "serving time" can have its productive moments. When Bob Maher was on the corporate side of human resources, he remembers interviewing a man who had a seven-year gap in his employment history. "He explained the gap by saying that he'd just gotten out of prison for killing his wife," says Maher. "While he was there, he'd developed some good job skills that he wanted to put to work."

After delving carefully into the man's past, Maher learned that the murder had been a crime of passion and that the man was considered completely rehabilitated. So, Maher—who appreciated the man's honesty—trusted his gut, hired the man and never regretted his decision.

Obviously, this is a high-risk interviewing strategy that should be used only as a last resort. In this particular case, it simply would not have been possible for this man to honestly explain (1) what he'd been doing for the past seven years and (2) how he acquired his expertise, without also mentioning his prison record.

A recovering alcoholic had developed a spotty employment record during an arduous three-year treatment program. To deal with that history, he had two choices: He could use a high-risk emotional strategy in which he identified himself as a recovering alcoholic and presented the issue as a "problem solved," or he could "cover his tracks" by focusing on the volunteer activities and skills he'd developed through his church involvements during this time.

There is no "right" or "wrong" way to handle such problems. The real key is to choose the strategy you feel best about—and to live comfortably with the consequences.

Terminations

Terminations are emotion-filled events that can make you feel angry, scared, nervous, humiliated or even relieved. Because unresolved emotions greatly hamper your ability to carry out an effective job-search campaign, most experts recommend a "feelings-first" approach.

In many cases, emotions that have been expressed and shared lose their power. Venting your feelings can offer a real cathartic value. After that, it becomes much easier to develop a rational, emotion-free explanation for your termination.

Why is this so important? Ed Goedert explains:

Attitude toward employers is the No. 1 thing I look at. Because so many people are losing their jobs, there's a lot more anger, resentment and cynicism toward

---

FOR YOUR INFORMATION

THE GOLDEN AX HALL OF FAME

Many people not only survive a job loss, they flourish afterward. To illustrate that point, Bob McCarthy, president of McCarthy Resources, Inc., in Los Angeles, created "The Golden Ax Hall of Fame," with awards to such notable victims of firings as Lee Iacocca, Winston Churchill, Benjamin Franklin, Albert Einstein, Henry Ford I and Alexander the Great. "Fifty percent of the time companies fire the wrong people," McCarthy says. "The process is so political."

---

employers. Corporations don't want to hire anyone who feels that way because those people are disruptive to the environment. They can't get along with their co-workers and they fight with their bosses.

If you're able to learn something about yourself (and your needs) from the experience, you can avoid repeating mistakes. But what kinds of lessons can be learned from such a painful experience?

Compassion. Humility. A new attitude toward risk. A better sense of your own needs and priorities. Even a newfound sense of power that evolves from knowing you survived the loss.

A marketing manager lost her job with a glamorous entrepreneurial cosmetics company when it was bought out by a pharmaceutical conglomerate. Her search for a new position took so long that she was forced to seek out consulting assignments. And while she missed having an organizational affiliation, the experience taught her how to be more visible, competitive, and professionally self-sufficient.

In another case, a Wall Street financial executive was constantly getting into power struggles with his supervisors and managed to antagonize almost every boss he ever had. Instead of quitting, he hung on until he got fired. Once out, he began to realize how much corporate life had been strangling him. He redirected his career into a smaller, more flexible organization and never had a major supervisory conflict again.

In such cases of mismatch, Patricia Berg, director of outplacement at Career Dynamics Inc. in Bloomfield, Minnesota, recommends introducing your references as a balancing point of view: "It invites the employer to recognize your current employment situation as a reflection of one person's opinion about you—not some objective reality."

Whatever you do, don't let the emotions of failure crowd out your memories of success. Most employers are less interested in the details of a termination than in how you've resolved or dealt with your feelings about the situation.

An executive vice president of a Fortune 100 company got fired because of a personality clash with his boss. Even though his termination was unrelated to performance, he found it painfully difficult to deal with the question, "Why did you leave your last employer?" Finally, to make his life easier, he decided to write a letter to CEOs explaining his firing up front. The letter began:

> Did you ever have a philosophical difference with your boss—and win?
> Me neither. And, I'm looking. . . .

Having cleared the way toward a more open and honest discussion of his situation helped this executive relax in the interview and present himself more confidently.

Qualifications

The bottom line is: Can you do the job? An employer who extends you a job offer believes you can.

When employers raise objections in the qualifications arena, it is usually because they perceive you as being overqualified (having too much experience), underqualified (having too little) or differently qualified. By knowing your product (yourself) and your market (their company), you should be able to anticipate and neutralize their objections with good sales technique.

Not Enough Experience

Janet Landay was hired into a newly created position as the director of exhibitions at the Glassell School in Houston, even though she'd never specifically done that kind of work before. She has, however, mastered the fine art of dealing with objections. When the director of the museum asked, "Why should I hire you? You've never been an exhibition director before," her response was immediate and direct:

Yes, but I have training in art history and experience in exhibitions, so this is a logical next step. I know I can do it. Besides, if it weren't new, it wouldn't be a challenge. And, if there weren't any challenge, why would I want the job?

Landay's "yes, but" strategy effectively neutralized the director's objection by selling related experience and potential. Apparently, the director was convinced. He offered her the job, which she readily accepted.

The ability to identify related experience or transferable skills is a crucial interviewing skill for the less-than-perfectly qualified.

Before Candy Gilmore became the director of outplacement services for The H.S. Group in Green Bay, Wisconsin, she had a strong (but wide-ranging) communications background that included lobbying for Fort Howard Corporation and managing the sales and marketing function for a hotel.

When she first considered the outplacement business, she knew almost nothing about the industry. To learn more, she did a lot of networking with human resources professionals and company presidents. In the process, she discovered that her diverse business background, teaching expertise and personal experience with transitions (her husband had lost his sales job and taken nine months to find a new one), made her a good candidate for the job. So when it came time to sell her skills, she knew exactly why she was qualified and what to emphasize. In her case, lots of up-front research on the industry proved invaluable for developing an effective interview strategy.

Sometimes, transferable skills are a little harder to identify. On paper, Carl Maxcey hardly looked like the perfect candidate for a job as a financial analyst with Shearson Lehman Hutton Inc. A tenured ethics professor at Loyola University in Chicago, he had no experience in the financial services industry whatsoever.

Yet he managed to convince then-staffing manager Lynn Lillibridge that he had the technical aptitude and personal drive to prosper in the securities industry. "We were impressed with Carl's discipline and determination," Ms. Lillibridge says. "He had accomplished so much in academia in such a short period of time, we were anxious to see if he could do it again with us."

So, what did Maxcey say that was so persuasive?

"I convinced them that teaching ethics to recalcitrant students was really no different than persuading skeptical clients to buy stocks," he says.

One final strategy relies heavily on a positive can-do attitude and your ability to demonstrate potential. With this method, you sell your exposure—in other words, "the fact that you've observed the task being done by others or worked closely with others who used that skill," says Tom Washington.

An analytical chemist in Texas interested in becoming a supervisor plans to use that strategy to "sell himself" into a management training position. He's thought carefully about the different supervisory styles he's experienced and can discuss what he liked and disliked about each particular style, as well as articulate how he'd synthesize those approaches into his own unique style. Only time will tell if this particular strategy proves effective for him.

The Wrong Degree

If an interviewer says, "I really wanted someone with a _____ degree," and you don't have one, there's no need to apologize. "I'm sorry I'm not what you're looking for" won't cut it as a reply, anyway. Instead, stress the strength and quality of what you do have with a "Yes, but" approach.

Remember, educational requirements aren't always cast in concrete. The fact that the employer is interviewing you at all means that he or she still considers you a viable candidate, even without the right degree.

After losing a long-standing position with a pharmaceutical company, a professional with 19 years of accounting experience (but no degree) addressed the issue by saying to employers, "Yes, I realize that a college degree is preferable. But I thought you wanted someone who could come in and handle your automated accounting systems. Let me tell you more about my accomplishments in that area . . ."

A banker sans MBA assured potential employers that he'd be more than happy to pursue an MBA with their assistance. This statement opened the door to a discussion of the company's attitude toward professional development.

A master's level psychologist was questioned about her lack of a doctorate. Since she felt strongly that more graduate school wasn't in her career scenario, she countered by asking, "What is it you think a PhD would do for me?"

Had the reply been "We want you to have more clinical experience," she was prepared to sell the experience she'd gathered in 10 years of private practice. But when the employer said, "We need someone who can obtain insurance reimbursement for our clients," she knew there was no rebuttal. The employer had a reason for wanting what he did. Unfortunately, that reason made her the wrong candidate for the job.

In some cases, a candidate may actually agree with the employer's objection. Patrice Becicka knew her lack of a college degree interfered with her feelings of professionalism although she loved her supervisory job at CCH Computax. When the facility closed, she seized the opportunity to finish her undergraduate degree more quickly.

For those who are struggling with a not-enough-education problem, there is one surefire way to overcome it: Get more education.

Overqualification

Jerry Hannigan has 25 years of marketing experience, including stints with Motorola, Gillette, Merrill Lynch, and most recently AT&T. In fact, his wealth of accumulated expertise often leads employers to remark "You seem overqualified."

Hannigan's initial reaction to such comments was to listen silently. Then he decided to rethink his job search strategy and prescreen positions more extensively on the telephone, but he still did nothing to directly address the objection.

If, like Hannigan, you've been accused of being overqualified, your first defense should be to reiterate your best qualifications for the position, says Phyllis Edelen, president of a human resources consulting firm in Gary, Indiana. You might say:

> I'm confused by your statement that I'm overqualified. I thought you wanted someone who could manage your marketing department. My 25 years of marketing experience demonstrate my ability to meet that challenge. For example, when I worked at _____, I repositioned the company's product line to increase revenues . . .

In other words, view the objection as another opportunity to sell your qualifications. This will push interviewers to rethink their objection and keep an open mind.

If the employer still seems to be waffling, Edelen recommends probing more deeply into the resistance.

> Is there something specific you're concerned about?

By inviting employers to express their reservations, you can open the door to a more fruitful discussion of what they really mean by "you're overqualified."

When Phyllis Ravin tried to move from self-employment to worker bee, employers used the overqualifications objection as a shorthand way of saying, "You may be used to being the boss, but I'm the boss here."

To neutralize this objection, Ravin (and others like her) could use Jim Kacena's four-step ARTS (Acknowledge, Redirect, Test, Story or Statement) approach for dealing with objections:

1. *Acknowledge.* Address the concern, but not the liability (e.g., "I can see where you might be concerned that I won't fit in").

2. *Redirect.* "It seems like you're looking for someone who's really a team player."

3. *Test.* "Is that your concern?"

4. *Story or Statement.* "Let me tell you about an experience I'm particularly proud of . . ." (then, relate a "team play" experience).

One caveat: Don't assume you understand the employer's objection. If you're at all unsure, ask for clarification lest you introduce a new liability by dealing with the wrong objection.

In Ravin's case, one employer made it clear that he thought she'd get bored and leave. Ravin tried to reassure him that a stable job with benefits was incentive enough for her, but he wasn't convinced. He offered her a salary plus commission job, hoping it would motivate her to work at top potential. She wasn't interested in that arrangement, so they called the whole deal off.

As Ravin discovered, people who just want to draw a steady paycheck and work 9 to 5 every day automatically raise red flags with employers who prefer candidates who will actively and enthusiastically work to make a contribution to their organization. To overcome this objection, Ravin needed to demonstrate a genuine enthusiasm for the organization and specific job responsibilities.

Ravin may also have underestimated how tedious the job might be for someone who's already accomplished so much more in her career. In other words, the employer may have raised a valid concern that she needs to face up to. Although moving back down the career ladder may seem to be an easy answer to a tough career question, downward moves are seldom as simple as they first appear.

"You're overqualified" can also mean that an employer doesn't really understand your qualifications. When Edward Buckbee decided to leave his academic career as a humanities professor at the University of Chicago for the world of banking, he spent a lot of time educating potential employers about the value of his Princeton PhD.

"People in business have a lot of preconceived notions about what academics really do for a living," he says. "They tend to think we're overeducated but lack common sense." As a result, they may be viewed as simultaneously over- and underqualified. In fact, they're simply differently qualified. The task is to convince employers that those skills count, too.

Compatibility

Diversity may be the buzzword for the 1990s, but many employers still prefer to hire in their own image. If you don't fit that particular mold, your task is to reassure them that you have "compatible differences."

Unfortunately, some interviewers show bad judgment when they evaluate candidates. Illegal questions are a perfect example. A recruiter with a Wall Street investment banking firm made headlines for asking MBA women, "Would you have an abortion to stay on the fast track?" Fortunately, the women banded together to get the recruiter fired. In another well-publicized case, a discount department store was called on the carpet for asking job applicants "How long can you hold you're urine?" Apparently, a weak bladder cannot be the final determinant of a candidates qualifications.

Not every illegal question is so flagrantly disrespectful. Many employers are simply concerned with how you'll fit into their environment. You do yourself a disservice if you automatically assume malicious intentions every time you hear an illegal question.

When Ann Moran, a 53-year-old former sales coordinator with AT&T, interviewed with a family-owned music company, she sensed that the interviewer was uncomfortable with the fact that she was black. Because she was interested in the job, she made a concerted effort to set the employer at ease by mentioning her experiences in all- or mostly white organizations.

Moran expects a certain amount of resistance because of her personal status. But she doesn't let it bother her too much. In fact, she quite enjoys the interviewing process. "I'm not desperate for a job. I know I have skills that employers can use. And I like meeting new people," Moran says. "That makes interviewing fun."

Part of her comfort comes from knowing what she will and won't tolerate. While interviewing with an Oklahoma-based company that was setting up shop in Indianapolis, one employer remarked: "I know I'm not supposed to ask you this, but I'm going to anyway. How old are you?"

Moran held her ground. "I'll answer that question after I get the job," she said. "Or even if I don't. But not now."

Her ploy worked because the employer followed up with an explanation of his question. "We've had something of a revolving door here," he told her. "And I really need to hire someone who plans to stay."

To which Moran responded: "I plan to work another 10 years."

Understanding the reservation beneath the question is often the key to an effective response.

When litigation attorney Nancy Hirsch interviewed for her current position, she was asked outright, "Do you plan to have a family?"

She knew the question was inappropriate; but her response indicates that she understood the employer's hesitation. "I'm very committed to my career," she said. "Even if I do have children, I still plan to work."

While it's important to know your rights, it's up to you whether you choose to enforce them.

FOR YOUR INFORMATION

KNOW YOUR RIGHTS

☆ Title VII of the Civil Rights Act of 1964 forbids employers from discriminating against any person on the basis of sex, race, age, national origin or religion.

☆ Title I of the Americans with Disabilities Act (1991) protects people with disabilities from discrimination in any aspect of employment, including application procedures, hiring, training, compensation, fringe benefits or promotion.

☆ The Age Discrimination in Employment Act (1967) prohibits discrimination in employment against workers age 40 or older and promotes employment of older workers.

"When dealing with an illegal question, it's important to know exactly where your boundaries are," says Patricia Berg.

For her, questions about family aren't off-limits. "Do you plan to have more children?" might have been a boundary in her childbearing years, but now she considers it a moot point.

When faced with an illegal question, you can:

1. Answer the question and hope the information isn't used against you.

2. Answer the question, then explore how the employer plans to use the information.

3. Ask how the information relates to the job requirements.

4. Refuse to answer the question.

The response you choose should be based on your own moral values and your desire to work for that organization. The use of illegal questions might, for example, cause you to reconsider your desire to work for the company. Or, you might want to make note of it and perhaps try to change the selection policies once you're hired.

If you decide you still want to work for the employer, you have to find a way to dismantle the objection, illegal or not.

Phyllis Edelen suggests asking for clarification: "I'm confused. I thought you wanted an experienced person who could make an immediate contribution to your organizational goals." (Then, convert the question into an opportunity to sell your skills for the position.)

Another strategy is to answer the question with a question.

Former Caremark executive assistant Diana Kraus always answers the "How old are you?" question with one of her own: "Can you tell me why this is a concern?"

She feels that it's important to explore the reasons behind the question so that she'll know if the environment really is wrong for her. "If it's a totally youthful environment, I don't want to work there, anyway," Kraus says. "I'd rather know before I take the job. Otherwise, I'll be unhappy later."

However tactlessly expressed, employers may have a legitimate concern about your commitment and energy level. To combat an ageist stereotype, a 61-year-old engineer with a 13-year-old son made sure employers knew he had no intention of retiring. By interviewing enthusiastically and persistently and proving to employers that "age is a state of mind," he landed a job within a scant three months.

Age, sex and race stereotypes are only three of the ways in which employers sometimes offend. But don't assume you know which one is at work.

When Phyllis Edelen was a corporate recruiter, she remembers working with a credit manager of a Fortune 500 company who never hired any of the black candidates she routed his way. When Edelen complained to her boss that the credit manager was racist, he responded:

"Send him a black Catholic and see what he does."

She complied, and shortly afterward the credit department had its first black employee. What looked like racial discrimination turned out to be religious discrimination instead!

Another example: An MIS professional was asked by a corporate recruiter: "Are you Jewish?" The man hesitated before he answered, "No. Why do you ask?"

"Because Jews are smart," the recruiter said. "Does that mean you're stupid?"

While illegal questions may indicate deep-seated prejudices, they can also reflect a more benign form of ignorance. Since they always mean "You're different. I don't know what to do with you," exploring the nature of that difference serves two important functions: First, it will make the employer more comfortable with you as a candidate; and second, it will give you more insight into the true nature of the organization.

You probably can't do much to change deeply rooted prejudices, but you can do a lot to resolve legitimate employment concerns—even if they're not legitimately expressed.

If you're offended by what you see and hear, you always have the right to say, "Thank you for your time, but I don't think this is the right place for me." If for no other reason than your own integrity, you decide where and how to plant your flag. But keep in mind that oversensitivity can easily turn into self-destructive pride.

5

Not-So-Typical Questions

S o far, we've dealt primarily with ways to anticipate and prepare for standard interview questions. Now I'd like to turn to three other types of questions, ranging from the highly relevant to the hopelessly irrelevant.

Problem-Solving Questions

Employers may present a real-life problem or hypothetical situation for you to try and solve.

In their search for a new associate for their small general practice firm, Oak Park, Illinois, attorneys Morris Seeskin and Eileen Fein asked candidates only two questions. Fein, who practices family law, gave candidates the facts from one of her family law cases, then asked them to come up with viable case strategies. Seeskin repeated this exercise using one of his civil practice cases.

Although applicants weren't expected to come up with a final solution, "We really wanted to know how the person would think about the problem, so we could see whether we felt comfortable with their style," Seeskin says.

One attorney, who'd been practicing law for two years, failed the test by responding that he hadn't studied family law since law school and didn't have a clue how to approach the case.

"You can tell a lot about people's thinking by the questions they ask," says Seeskin. "This guy failed to come up with a single question that would help him solve the problem."

From that encounter, Seeskin and Fein knew the candidate would never be resourceful enough to handle their diverse caseload.

Dick Knowles, a consultant with J.K. Knowles Construction Inc. in Chatauqua, New York, likes to present hypothetical situations to engineers and technical people. For example, he might ask a construction engineer, "What would you do if your crew was digging underground and they ran into rock?"

Such questions are valuable, Knowles says, because they allow him to see people think right in front of him. He adds, "I've found that it gives me a more accurate evaluation tool, which means that there's a better chance that things will work out in the long run. Otherwise, we end up having to fire people. Why put everyone through that if it isn't necessary?"

Bob McCarthy applauds this new trend toward "scenario questions," in which candidates are asked to think through a problem in front of the interviewer. "It makes it real because you get to see how people work, rather than just listening to them tell you how they work," he says.

Aficionados of this technique often rely on the "in-basket exercise," in which they take a piece of paper from their in-basket, read it aloud, then ask the candidate how he or she would handle it.

During one interview, Jerry Hannigan was asked to solve three different marketing problems. Hannigan believes that the questions were only partly asked to test his expertise. "Actually, I think he wanted some free marketing advice for some problems he was struggling with," Hannigan says. "But it didn't make me feel exploited; it was nice to be able to demonstrate what I know how to do rather than endlessly talking about it."

For the most part, this interview format requires a shift in emphasis from finding the "right" answers to showing you know the right way to come up with answers. Linda C. Jones, an industrial psychologist with outplacement firm King Chapman Broussard & Gallagher's Denver office suggests the following five-step process for dealing with problem-solving questions:

1. Listen intently to what's being asked.

2. Ask clarifying questions to determine exactly what the interviewer is looking for.

3. Respond by first explaining how you'd gather the data necessary to make an informed decision.

4. Discuss how you'd use that data to generate options.

5. Finally, based on the data you've gathered, the available options, and your understanding of the open position, explain how you'd make an appropriate decision or recommendation.

In the Introduction, I described Monica Tulley's experience with the interviewer who demanded: "Sell me this watch."
Using Jones's process, the situation could be handled as follows:

1. Clarify whether the employer has established an intended market, and if so, who the company has targeted.

2. Determine the watch's best features and how they're beneficial to this market.

3. Discuss how to obtain this information (focus groups, telemarketing surveys, etc.) if the interviewer can't provide it (which, of course, he can't because he hasn't given her a real product to sell).

4. Discuss ways that this data could be used to develop effective selling strategies.

5. Finally, explain how to select a selling strategy based on the information received.

In other words, she'd communicate that a lot of up-front work must be done before a product can be properly sold!

This method would also work well with other questions, such as this one, which Standard Control Co. executives routinely use when interviewing prospective human resources directors: "What would be your approach (from an HR point of view) to opening a new plant?"

Many situational questions are set up to explore the issue of "fit." The interviewer wants to know if the way you think about—and handle—the problem or situation is consistent with the way the rest of their group operates.

Rick Ehlers, president of The Corporate Network in Hoffman Estates, Illinois, remembers working with a candidate who was interviewing for a sales position with a young and aggressive computer services company. The hiring manager posed the following situational question:

> We are sending you on an assignment to Carmel, California. You have an unlimited expense account. What kind of car are you going to rent?

The candidate knew the question was a test. But, of what? His frivolity with other people's money? His taste in cars? Or something else?

He thought about the company: the image that it clearly wanted to project as a brash, up-and-coming, go-getter in the marketplace. He thought about his hypothetical assignment. After all, he reasoned, things are a little looser in California. And he formulated his response: A Porsche!

Later on he discovered that the three candidates who passed the "car test" had been bold enough to rent Porsches, Ferraris and Jaguars.

One well-meaning candidate (who tried to save his future employer money by renting a Honda Accord) was definitely out on his ear. Ditto for the unfortunate applicant who preferred to drive a Mercedes-Benz. Although the latter candidate managed to get the price range right, he blew it on the image front.

While problem-solving questions always have a "How would you handle?" or "What would you do if?" theme, some questions are designed to reveal your character or values.

One human resources manager was asked: "What would you do if one of your employees came to you with knowledge that the company president was having an affair with a secretary?"

A Dartmouth graduate who was interviewing for a rookie cop position got "zinged twice" with questions of ethics. First, he was asked: "What would you do if you pulled a drunk driver over for a traffic violation and it turned out to be your mother?" Later, he was asked what he'd do if he saw his sargeant pocket a knife from a crime scene.

Both questions obviously reflect an interest in knowing how the candidate personally deals with sensitive legal issues. But there is no "right" answer. There is only your answer. And, sometimes the hardest thing of all is to stand up for your beliefs, knowing that it might cost you the job.

When Roger Gilman, a professor of morality and ethics at Northeastern Illinois University in Chicago, first interviewed for his current position, a prospective co-worker questioned him closely about his grading practices. From the interviewer's tone of voice, Gilman inferred that the man preferred instructors with lenient policies.

Gilman, who considers himself a "hard-but-fair" evaluator, didn't cave in to the interviewer's pressure. "I could've told him what he wanted to hear. But it wouldn't have been true. And even though I wanted the job, I didn't want to lie to get it," Gilman says. "If I didn't get hired because I told the truth, I wouldn't have been happy there, anyway."

As it turns out, the professor had been trying to trick Gilman into admitting he was a "soft touch." The interviewer believed many of his co-workers were too easy on students, and he was determined to weed out future offenders.

Although this particular story has a happy ending (Gilman got the job), it might easily have played out differently. Had he fallen into the trap of saying what he thought the interviewer wanted to hear, he probably wouldn't have been offered the position.

Behavior-Based Questions

Some questions are based on the assumption that past behavior is the best predictor of future performance. Phrased as declaratives, they usually begin with the words "Tell me about a time when . . . ," "Describe a time when you . . ." or "Give me an example of a time when . . ."

Behavior-based interviewers usually develop their questions around the traits and skills they deem necessary for succeeding in the position or organization. For example, an interviewer for a job that included lots of customer service would undoubtedly ask, "Tell me about a time when you had to deal with an irate customer."

Some candidates find the format of the question unsettling. In the pressure of the moment, they simply can't think of a single thing. To overcome that obstacle, Tom Washington recommends developing a list of experiences that cover the waterfront of skills and characteristics required for the position you seek.

You can handle this most expediently by developing responses to standard questions that always include at least one illustrative example. Since it helps to tell stories to anchor information, anyway, you can be ready for both eventualities by preparing in this manner.

At times, behavior-based questions are nothing more than standard questions in a slightly different frame. In these cases, you can use a strategy much like your standard interview style.

For example, should an interviewer say, "Tell me about a time when you had a conflict with a supervisor," you can begin by clarifying the question (e.g., "Would you like me to discuss my relationship with my last supervisor?"). If you get an affirmative nod, go on to describe your relationship with that supervisor.

If this description raises any negatives, be sure to follow up by explaining what you learned from the experience. Keep in mind that half the questions behavior-based interviewers ask are phrased negatively. To avoid the trap, remember that you must respond to every question by revealing a strength, and without getting so flustered that you deal your hand away.

Says Tom Washington: "Whenever you speak, your intention should be to sell yourself, not merely to answer questions. Try not to forget your primary purpose."

Sometimes you'll have trouble coming up with a specific experience. Since behavior-based interviewers can be like bulldogs who won't give up until they get the specifics they want, you may have to encourage them to ask their questions differently.

For example, if asked to describe a time when you failed, you might reply, "I need you to help me out here. Since I tend to view most things as an opportunity to learn, I'm not sure I know what you mean by the term 'failure.' If you learn something from an experience, it can never be a failure. And I try to learn from everything I do. Would you like me to share a learning experience with you?"

Whenever you do share an experience (and in this interviewing format, you'll share lots of them), make sure that everything you say and do reflects positively on you.

Let me give you a personal example: If I were asked to describe a time when I had to take a stand on an unpopular position, I'd probably talk about my graduate school advisor, who believed that master's-level psychologists like me shouldn't go into private practice because they needed more clinical experience. I agreed that more supervision would help, but I felt that if I could use my entrepreneurial skills to develop a client base, I could also afford to purchase the services of a quality supervisor. So I did. The end result was that I received clinical supervision from one of the most competent psychologists in the city—and it was someone whom I'd hand-selected to teach me.

I believe that this example demonstrates my willingness to go against conventional wisdom without sacrificing my personal integrity or professional development. But I wouldn't leave it up to the interviewer to figure that out. Rather than simply tell the story and hope the interviewer would get the point, I'd use Laurie Anderson's strategy (described in Chapter 2) of saying, "I tell you this story because . . ." In addition, I'd follow it up with some kind of a feedback question to determine how the interviewer was processing the message: "I'm curious about your reaction to my story. Is that what you wanted to hear?"

You can also follow up with a turnabout strategy. For example, in response to the question, "Describe a time when you had to fire someone," you might follow up your response with a question of your own: "Can you tell me more about the employees that I'd be supervising in this position? Do you often have to let people go? If so, how do you usually handle it?"

Sometimes, interviewers may try to bully you into endless specific examples. However, you can't be expected to have had every kind of experience in the universe. Sometimes, the only true answer is, "I'm sorry. Nothing comes to mind." If, for example, an interviewer should ask me, "Tell me about a time when you lost your temper," I could honestly say, "I do get angry sometimes but I never lose my temper. In fact, I'm not sure I have a temper."

All these strategies use the following basic principles:

☆ Just because you are anxious to comply with the question, don't tell stories that will hurt you. Always remember that your stories must serve the purpose of selling you.

☆ If you really don't understand the question (or want to buy some time to formulate an answer), ask for clarification: "Can you be more specific? I'm not sure I understand what you are looking for."

☆ Once you've told your story, explain what you hoped to show with it, rather than assume the interviewer got your point.

☆ Ask for feedback. Find out how the interviewer is processing the response you gave. This will enable you to correct any misconceptions and clarify meanings.

☆ Remember you don't have to answer every question just because it was asked. Sometimes the only right answer is "I don't know."

FOR YOUR INFORMATION

THE 25 MOST POPULAR BEHAVIOR-BASED QUESTIONS

Tell me about a time when you . . .

1. Worked effectively under pressure.
2. Handled a difficult situation with a co-worker.
3. Were creative in solving a problem.
4. Missed an obvious solution to a problem.
5. Were unable to complete a project on time.
6. Persuaded team members to do things your way.
7. Wrote a report that was well-received.
8. Anticipated potential problems and developed preventive measures.
9. Had to make an important decision with limited facts.
10. Were forced to make an unpopular decision.
11. Had to adapt to a difficult situation.
12. Were tolerant of an opinion that was different from yours.
13. Were disappointed in your behavior.
14. Used your political savvy to push a program through that you really believed in.
15. Had to deal with an irate customer.
16. Delegated a project effectively.
17. Surmounted a major obstacle.
18. Set your sights too high (or too low).
19. Prioritized the elements of a complicated project.
20. Got bogged down in the details of a project.
21. Lost (or won) an important contract.
22. Made a bad decision.
23. Had to fire a friend.
24. Hired (or fired) the wrong person.
25. Turned down a good job.

☆ Don't be so intimidated by the format that you're afraid to have some fun with it.

If you're a highly experienced person who can organize your thoughts and strategy quickly, you can have a great time creating perfectly tailored responses: "Based on my understanding of your organization, I should probably tell you about the time when . . ."

To get to that point, though, you'll need to do lots of up-front thinking about the examples you want to use. You may also need some props to help you. Your resume may be the single best prop you can find in the heat of the moment. If you've taken the time to develop accomplishment statements, a quick skim will remind you exactly what you've been doing all these years. You can also use notes, but try not to rely on them too much. Instead, jot down a few memory joggers that will quickly remind you of certain stories.

Visuals are another possibility. If you have a portfolio or work samples with you, you can always say, "Rather than talking in generalities, let me show you exactly what I did." Then you can save your breath by letting your work speak for you.

Unrelated Questions

Some questions rely on an untrained psychologist to make psychological interpretations, and, as a result, their usefulness is highly suspect.

Jim Kacena remembers working with a displaced executive who was asked, "If you were stranded on a desert island and could only have one other person with you, who would it be?"

In an attempt to show love and loyalty, some people would say their spouse.

Others might pick a fantasy lover—say, Meg Ryan or Tom Cruise—seeing solitude as an opportunity for an exciting sexual rendezvous. Adolescent, maybe; but does it really mean you'd make a bad business executive?

Fortunately, the candidate who was asked to play out this Robinson Crusoe fantasy opted to be stranded with a boatbuilder, and in the process demonstrated his resourcefulness.

However irrelevant a question may seem, you can do your best to make it relevant by making sure that your answer reveals something positive about your character or work performance. Don't get seduced into the game and forget why you're there in the first place.

A capital equipment salesman was particularly effective at converting seemingly obscure questions into opportunities to display his qualifications.

When confronted by a human resources representative with the following one-two punch: "What characteristics did you learn from your mother?" and "How about your father?", the 42-year-old candidate responded:

> From my mother, I learned to have confidence in myself—that I can do anything I set my mind to. From my father, I learned the value of persistence.

By marrying the qualities of self-confidence and persistence, he conveyed to the recruiter that he had two character traits that would also make him effective in the sales role he was pursuing.

But he wasn't content to let the recruiter passively process the information he provided. Instead, he followed up with a question of his own:

"I'm curious what you're looking for in that question?"

Unfortunately, the recruiter didn't have a good rationale for her selection strategy.

"I'm not sure," she said. "But someone asked me that question in an interview once and I liked it. So, now I ask it all the time."

Her flimsy response notwithstanding, it always makes sense to check out how the interviewer is processing your response so that you won't be misinterpreted. Otherwise, there's no telling what someone might do with that particular information.

For example, should you be asked the favorite of Barbara Walters: "If you could be any kind of tree, what would it be?" your response might be "I'd like to be an oak tree. Does that mean I'm strong and proud?" Or you can provide the interpretation yourself: "I think I'd like to be a cherry tree in blossom because they're so lively and attractive." (However, you wouldn't want to say, "I'd probably be a weeping willow because I'm depressed and cry a lot.")

One of the best answers I've heard to this question came from a laid-off facilities manager who responded by asking, "What kind of trees do you hire?"

To the question, "If you could be any kind of animal, what would it be?" my personal preference is to say "I think I'd like to be a human being."

In some cases, the questions aren't so much a test of imagination (or a misguided attempt to interpret your psychology) as an interviewer's search for clues to compatibility.

When Candy Gilmore interviewed with Fort Howard Corporation, she was asked, "What is your position on nuclear disarmament?" Knowing that it was a "fit" question, she chose a middle-of-the-road answer that wouldn't antagonize anyone.

In that same interview, she was also asked, "What kind of bridge player are you?" as a way of determining her competitiveness.

If you can figure out that competitiveness is the issue at stake, you can answer the real question beneath the question. Sometimes, however, the phrasing of the question makes it too obscure to figure out.

Rather than second-guess the interviewer's motives, you can always say: "Can you tell me how this relates to the position?" which is a way of asking politely, "Do I need to play bridge to work for you?" This tactic may surface the concern more directly.

"What's your favorite movie" or "What's the last book you read?" also fall into the "What do they really want me to say?" category. Again, don't let the questions throw you off. Sometimes, an interviewer is more interested in how you respond than what you actually say.

After being asked, "Did you see the movie *Batman?*" one candidate replied, "No, I didn't."

This innocuous enough exchange resulted in an interviewing tirade. "I can't believe you haven't seen *Batman!*" the interviewer fumed. "Don't you know it's already grossed $15 million? It's the most popular movie around. How could you not have seen it?"

The candidate didn't lose her cool. "I didn't see it," she said. "What do you want me to do—lie?"

Apparently, that was the right answer because the interviewer warmed up considerably after her response. His outrage, it seems, was staged to gauge her response to irrational bosses.

He might have been happy with her, but what does that tell you about the office environment she might encounter? This might be a good time to ask more questions about the seemingly temperamental people she'd be working for.

While you never want to be rude, it doesn't hurt to hold interviewers accountable for the questions they expect you to answer. It may even make them think twice before asking those questions again.

"What we're looking for is someone with a keen memory for details."

6

Want to Dance? The Psychology of Interviewing

A highly competent actuary lost his job with a major insurance company during a reorganization. Since he was the sole wage earner for his family, and his wife was pregnant with their fourth child, he was obviously concerned (but not panicked) about finding a new job. To add to his plight, he was a British citizen here on a work visa. Unless he found another employer to sponsor him within six months, he and his family would have to leave the country.

Given that sobering situation, it's not surprising that this man—who under other circumstances has a wonderfully dry wit—came across rather stone-faced during interviews. When he asked for feedback from one hiring manager who rejected his employment bid, the manager commented that he was "just too intense."

The Value of Good Rapport

You don't have to be a witty conversationalist to get job offers. But by making a concerted effort to warm things up with good rapport, you'll make interviewers feel more emotionally comfortable with their decision and, in the process, reduce their fear of making a costly hiring mistake.

Generally, the more at home you are with yourself, the more successful you'll be at open and honest communications.

Certainly this proved true for Mike Murphy, a former district sales manager with Hoover Company, who has been able to use personal information to his advantage many times.

Murphy remembers one particularly spectacular experience with a hiring manager from Mutual of New York. The interview was moving along laconically until the manager asked whether Murphy played golf.

"After he heard I was a scratch golfer, he seemed a lot more interested in me," Murphy marvels. "A lot more interested."

It isn't Murphy's great golf game that's at issue here. It's more his willingness to enter into the interview conversation wholeheartedly. This apparently impressed the interviewer enough to help him get to the next level. It also helps greatly that Murphy feels he has nothing to hide. In addition to a stable work history, he's in his early 30s, enjoys good health, and a good marriage, and is expecting his first child.

Viewed from another angle, however, he might just as easily feel insecure and defensive because he was laid off, has no prior experience in his new career of choice (financial planning) and never completed college.

But he doesn't see it that way. Rather than focusing on his liabilities, he's upbeat and positive about his skills and future. That enthusiasm seems to be contagious; despite his lack of experience in financial services, he managed to generate a dozen interviews in the first three weeks of his job search.

California consultant Bob McCarthy remembers a similarly exciting interview with a managing partner of Coopers & Lybrand for an about-to-be-created position of outplacement director. A few minutes into the interview, the partner received an emergency phone call, giving McCarthy the opportunity to relax and observe his surroundings.

When the phone call was over, McCarthy commented that he, too, collected Western American art. From there, the men launched into an enthusiastic discussion of their common passion—a conversation that McCarthy believes clinched him the job offer.

"He already knew I had the technical skills to do the job or I wouldn't have been sitting there in his office," McCarthy says. "But after that conversation, he knew that I was also someone he'd enjoy working with."

An architect in Indiana showcased his woodworking hobby when he brought his architectural drawings to an interview in a beautifully handcarved box.

The employer was so impressed with the candidate's woodworking skills that he asked him to "bring that beautiful box back with you on your next visit."

Six months into his new job, the architect learned that his handcarved box actually got him hired. It was *the* one thing that truly made him stand out from the other candidates.

You can add value to your candidacy by using personal information (in the form of shared interests) to generate rapport with the interviewer. But many seasoned executives don't feel comfortable enough to join in such lighthearted banter. (In one memorable case, a job hunter was so unsure of his role that he never even referred to the fact that his interviewer was in a body cast.) For them, the interview feels like a life-or-death situation.

"Lots of interviewees psych themselves wrong," says career counselor Irene Mendelson. "They get so worried about being rejected that they never take the initiative to establish a bond."

There's always a temptation to see yourself in a one-down situation during interviews. After all, the interviewer is sitting on the throne of power.

The result can be stultifying. But don't lose sight of the fact that interviewers may be equally insecure. Like you, they are human beings who come encumbered with their own emotional baggage.

When Mickey Allweiss first started interviewing potential associates, he found himself spending way too much time and energy trying to convince candidates to come and work for him.

"I was trying to sell them on the firm, instead of the other way around," he admits. "It got in the way of my ability to evaluate their qualifications objectively."

Allweiss isn't alone. Lots of candidates have been on the receiving end of employers who spend more time talking about themselves than exploring the candidate's credentials.

Depending on our frame of mind, this can be a frustration or a relief. In fact, it presents a relationship problem. It may let you off the hook (temporarily) in terms of selling yourself, but if you walk out the door and the employer doesn't know what you can do, you probably won't get called back for another interview.

A shipping supervisor remembers being thoroughly annoyed with a hiring manager who wouldn't let her get a word in edgewise. He was too busy bragging about himself. She got her "just revenge" when he made the mistake of asking her "How old do you thing I am?" The candidate took a notch off the man's ego by adding five years to his age.

Fortunately, he didn't hold it against her; but there was an awkward moment when he ran a distracted hand through his graying hair and asked "Really? That old?"

In general, your goal should be to do your best to nurture and develop a budding relationship with the interviewer. This won't always be easy. At times, it may call for some true social grace.

A corporate social worker recalls interviewing the head of a private Employee Assistance Program manager who showed up 30 minutes late for their scheduled interview. The social worker was annoyed; but she did her best to maintain her composure.

Her mood didn't improve when the interviewer made it clear that he hadn't prepared for her interview. "I didn't have time to read your resume," he greeted her. "Why don't you just tell me about yourself?"

If you haven't read my resume, she thought, how do you know you want to interview me? But she kept her thoughts to herself and launched in gamely with her prepared text. After about two minutes, the interviewer interrupted her abruptly to take a phone call. At that point, she realized that it would be impossible to gain the man's attention in any meaningful way.

Without trying to offend him, she suggested that they reschedule to a time that was more convenient for him. To which he responded: "Every day is like this."

Picking up the cue, she replied: "It sounds like you really need some extra help."

"I'm swamped," he replied. "I apologize. Let me do one more thing and then I'll ask my secretary to hold my calls."

After that, he did manage to keep the interruptions to a minimum.

In retrospect, we can see that the social worker's ability to assert some control over the situation without antagonizing her potential employer proved to be the winning ticket. In fact, her ability to empathize with his situation enabled him to be more open and receptive to her.

By trying to understand and put his needs first, the social worker opened the door to better communication and, perhaps, even showcased one of her counseling/social work skills.

Granted, this may not always be easy. But if you can learn to view these difficult situations as an interviewing challenge rather than a personal affront, you'll definitely grow more comfortable in the interviewing role.

Admittedly, becoming a stellar interviewee may not be your No. 1 career goal. But any time you're in the job market, it will be a skill that you'll feel grateful to have mastered.

Deal with Your Emotions First

It takes a certain level of self-confidence and emotional resiliency to participate wholeheartedly in interviews. Unfortunately, many job hunters start interviewing before they're on stable emotional ground.

Oklahoma career consultant Joy Reed-Belt remembers interviewing a bank executive who was laid off from his asset-based lending position after 27 years, when his employer made a strategic decision to focus in another direction.

Since he was on the job market through no fault of his own (and was already six months into his job search), Reed-Belt assumed it was an innocuous question when she asked, "Why did you leave the bank?"

To her amazement, the man's eyes teared up as he started rummaging frantically in his briefcase for something. Watching his desperation, the few minutes that it took him to find what he was looking for seemed an eternity.

Finally, he produced a letter from the bank explaining why he'd lost his job and dropped it on her desk. As she read it over, he said, "Can you believe they did this to me?" Then he turned his back to her and started crying.

"I felt so sorry for him," Reed-Belt says. "He wasn't getting over his loss and on with his life. But I couldn't recommend him for the position. He just wasn't emotionally ready to make another employment commitment."

While honesty and candor can really enhance interview rapport, interviewers aren't usually inspired to hire people who evoke their sympathy—however sympathetic they may feel. If you feel overwhelmed emotionally, you'll need to work through those conflicts first. Otherwise, you'll wash away career opportunities with your tears.

"After a job loss, people need to reconnect with themselves," says CareerLabs counselor Linda Bougie. "They need to articulate and clarify what they want. Working through values and conflicts is a way of taking back control."

Career failures (in the form of firings, layoffs and poor performance reviews) do require some extra emotional effort to resolve. To those who fall into that category, NYU philosophy professor Joshua Halberstam offers the advice summarized in the following sections.

Be Honest

Start by being honest with yourself. You aren't doing yourself a favor by pretending that a failure never happened. Even if you finesse the interview, self-deception has a way of catching up with you.

Take, for example, the case of a communications executive who was laid off after 12 successful years with Sears, Roebuck & Company. Feeling miserably abandoned, he immediately jumped to another position rather than deal with his feelings of rejection. After six months, he realized the job was well beneath his abilities, so he changed positions again. However, he never mentioned his six-month post-Sears stint to his new employer because he was afraid of looking like a job-hopper. When it was discovered that the executive had lied about his work history, he was dismissed.

Had the executive dealt with his anxiety at separating from Sears, he wouldn't have compounded his problem so dramatically. Instead, he created a work history that really did require a lot more explanation.

Learn How to Perceive Failure

Understand that failure isn't a definitive measure of your abilities. It only measures how well you performed under those particular circumstances, or in that particular setting. Be careful about generalizing your failures to all situations. (For those of you whose layoff is unrelated to performance, it may be equally important to differentiate between a real failure and a perception that you've failed.)

Explain Your Failure

Offer an explanation (not an excuse) for your lack of success. It won't help your cause to blame others for failure. If you did indeed contribute to the problem, own up to your responsibility. It will help point to a more positive side of your character—your willingness to be accountable.

While working at Crossway Community Center in the Washington, D.C., area, Patricia Haskell interviewed a candidate who spent several minutes complaining about her former employer as a lead-in to why she was looking for a new job. If the interviewee was looking for sympathy, it didn't work. "It just made me question her professionalism," Haskell says. "And it certainly didn't do anything to convince me to hire her for our agency."

Describe What You Learned from the Failure

Point to an improvement trend that shows the problem probably won't recur. Says Suzanne Jenniches, manager of systems and technology operations for Westinghouse Electronic Systems Group: "Anyone who expects a perfect career without any mistakes or failures is definitely headed for disillusionment because there is no such thing. The important fact isn't whether you make mistakes, but that you have the capacity to learn from those errors so they won't be repeated in the future."

Monica Tulley relates the story of one client who was a counselor in a hospital. Although the woman was a truly empathic therapist with great counseling skills, she wasn't much on paperwork and her performance evaluations reflected this. However, the therapist failed to take her employer's complaints seriously and was subsequently "let go" for that failure. With 20-20 hindsight, she realizes she should have taken the paperwork complaint more seriously, and in the future, she'll undoubtedly do so.

There is, of course, another solution—which leads us to Professor Halberstam's final point.

Consider a Career Adjustment

Sometimes, you fail in a job because it was a mismatch, either in terms of skills, personality or values. Realizing that can inspire you to reexamine your career direction.

A highly successful advertising sales manager developed a brain tumor at age 40. Not surprisingly, his sales dipped that year. But even the following year, after he'd recovered physically, his sales remained well below par. At first, the sales manager thought it was due to some residual damage from his surgery, but as time went on, he realized that his priorities had changed. Faced with a premature awareness of his own mortality, he no longer thrived on the challenge of "closing the deal." Softer goals, such as helping people and making a contribution, had surfaced and, with them, a need for a new career.

A career counselor helped him work through his feelings about his abilities, values, and future and he identified the field of sales training as a viable and potentially more satisfying alternative. This process enabled him to overcome his lethargy and defeatist attitudes about his career in order to sell himself with renewed vigor and enthusiasm.

Take Time to Heal

Emotional recoveries like this take time, determination and support. "When your self-esteem is battered, self-promotion is always a problem," says Linda Bougie. "People need to do a lot of front-end work to get past that point."

For one distribution center manager, participation in an outplacement workshop ushered in the beginning of a psychological and emotional healing. Having grown up (professionally speaking) with one employer, the manager was an "accidental careerist" who, having started out as a mailroom clerk 17 years earlier, had worked her way up to managing distributions for 32 branch offices and 4,000 professional clients.

Since she'd never really tried to look at her skills and accomplishments apart from her specific job responsibilities, she lacked a vocabulary to describe what she knew how to do, and until she learned that new language she could hardly be expected to "sell herself" to new employers.

The distribution center manager had been truly happy with her employer, and would gladly have lived out her career there. But when the company made a strategic decision to close its Midwest facility, she no longer had that option. Although it wasn't personal, she took their decision personally and hard. For weeks afterward, she couldn't go anywhere near her old office and questioned whether she even wanted to work again.

Like the process many people go through after the death or divorce of a loved one, the discovery of a professional identity apart from an employment mate required this woman's time and effort.

The resume-writing process can be a concrete and practical way to look at your contributions more objectively. Remembering back can help you regain your equilibrium, focus on what you did right and begin to place the employment experience in a different perspective—as one event in a career, rather than a not-so-grand finale.

Lots of experienced professionals tend to focus on the negatives in their situation without realizing that those negatives may be more perception than reality.

A 58-year-old sales manager was overwhelmingly distressed about his layoff from a major floor-care company. He didn't have enough retirement benefits to retire and was convinced no one would hire him. Like many of his peers, he'd bought into the myth that at a certain age no one wants you anymore.

Because he felt defensive about his age, he had trouble focusing on his genuine strengths. Not only was he a productive employee with a proven track record of sales and management accomplishments, he also carried with him a host of connections that savvy employers could easily convert into new business. Finally, the benefits he carried made him an affordable candidate. But until he learned to recognize those genuine strengths, he could hardly be expected to convince others that he had them.

Preparation, the experts agree, is the key.

"Preparation helps you manage the anxiety because it gives you something concrete and productive to focus on," says Dennis Huebschman, an executive vice president with Nelson, Harper and Associates, a Phoenix-based outplacement firm.

Support systems are equally valuable because they can help buffer your self-esteem against rejection. For the distribution center manager, her long-standing network of (now former) co-workers, clients, vendors and suppliers became a real source of comfort. Their willingness to support her and refer her to potential employers gave her more credibility with herself. Her self-esteem soared, and she began to believe she might actually find another job that wasn't entry-level.

Once your self-esteem issues are under control, it's much easier to establish effective interview communications. But if you feel too meek for the arduous task of self-promotion, clam up defensively at employers' questions, or insist on getting drunk at lunch to ease your anxiety, you just aren't ready to tackle interviewing properly yet.

Also, don't feel you have to share a common passion for golf or Western art with the interviewer to succeed. You just have to show a genuine interest in the employer and the employer's organization. That requires the ability to listen as well as talk.

FOR YOUR INFORMATION

Listen Up!

We have two ears and one mouth so that we may hear twice as much as we speak.
—Epictetus (ca) A.D. 55–135

Develop Your Listening Skills

"No one is born with great listening skills, and cultivating them isn't always easy," says Donald Sweet, a human resources consultant in Ridgewood, N.J. He recommends several guidelines that are described in the following sections.

Don't Be Preoccupied with Your Own Ideas and Opinions

No matter how eager you are to show off your skills and homework, interviews are meant to involve lots of give-and-take. You shouldn't be the only speaker at the meeting.

As part of a search committee for the executive director of a nonprofit organization, Reed-Belt remembers interviewing one candidate who felt compelled to impose his own structure and agenda on the process. During a momentary pause, the interviewee seized the opportunity to ask if he could make a formal presentation, to which the stunned interviewers assented.

"Although we were impressed with how much homework he'd done, it did raise the question of flexibility and fit," Reed-Belt says. "He seemed to really need to do things his own way."

Give Your Complete Attention to the Interviewer

When you concentrate on the interviewer's words, you'll seem more genuinely interested in the position. This means learning to listen for "intent" as well as "content."

It's especially important to listen for "buy signals," according to Jim Kacena. "If they offer to show you around the office, introduce you to the other people, or ask when you're available to start, these are all 'buy signals' that mean the interviewer is warming up to you," says Kacena. "They usually mean that you're on the right track."

Restrain Your Individual Sensitivities or Biases

Prejudice is the hallmark of a closed mind, and hence the enemy of good listening. It leads otherwise intelligent people straight into a host of misunderstandings and missed opportunities.

In an interview with a female executive, a 53-year-old real-estate developer who truly believed "a woman's place is in the home" was asked about his relationships with bosses, co-workers and subordinates. Had a male interviewer posed the same questions, the candidate undoubtedly would have heard and responded to them differently. But because they were initiated by a woman, he refused to take them (or her) seriously. He replied with a series of sexual innuendoes and flirtatious come-ons that the interviewer found totally offensive and inappropriate. She, in turn, had the last laugh when she refused to take him seriously either.

You don't have to turn yourself upside down and inside out to rid yourself of basic prejudice. You just need to be aware of your biases and consciously set them aside. Then, perhaps, you'll be able to hear what the other person is trying to say.

Don't Jump to Conclusions

People who fear rejection sometimes try to seize control by doing the rejecting first. A computer programmer with a very iffy track record (which made her acutely sensitive to criticism) was always quick to identify interviewer incompetence and unprofessionalism because it gave her the power to reject them first.

"People who have been fired or laid off often feel like they've been kicked out of the corporate family," says Reed-Belt. "When the interview becomes a search for another employment mate to validate and accept them, the situation becomes emotionally overloaded. It's like being naked—and here's this employer you've never met before inspecting your worthwhileness. It's very demoralizing."

In many cases, people counteract that feeling of neediness by becoming very judgmental. This behavior may feel emotionally safe, but it's not likely to encourage job offers.

Try to Keep an Open Mind

No place is perfect, so avoid hasty assessments. A troubled publicist was an avid member of the Groucho Marx ("I wouldn't want to be a member of any club that would have me in it") fan club; she was quick to find fault with every employer who interviewed her. Although this would temporarily make her feel better about herself, eventually her lack of job offers hurt her self-esteem and even began to make her "interview phobic."

Focus on Interviewer Needs, Not Your Own

Don't try too hard to impress interviewers with your expertise. While showing off with lots of technical jargon may make you feel smart, this approach often backfires because the interviewer doesn't have a clue what you're talking about. Make a sincere effort to communicate; speak the interviewer's language.

Before job interviews, Patrice Becicka makes a conscious decision whether to use "tax," "computer software" or "management" language.

"If I'm talking to another tax person, I can say I managed the electronic filing department," Becicka says. "But that function is meaningless to nontax people. It just makes me look like what I do is so different from what they do."

Communication is especially critical if you're not a native English speaker. You may need to slow down the tempo of your speech (to adjust for your accent), or check in periodically with the interviewer to make sure you're communicating clearly. (Astute observers can also detect the glazed-over look that appears in interviewers' eyes when they don't "get it.")

In any event, interviewees who insist on using a communication style that screams "stranger in a strange land" shouldn't be surprised when they remain outsiders.

Know Your Own Needs and Values

There's a flip side to this equation. A systems analyst who's been consistently frustrated in his career because of his manager's lack of technical expertise makes a point of "talking shop" with hiring managers. When he interviews with other "computer junkies," this approach makes him a stimulating and exciting candidate.

Toward those who can't understand him (and therefore probably won't hire him), he takes a philosophical "I probably wouldn't want to work there, anyway" stance.

Prepare Thoughtful Questions

Good questions help you determine whether you have the skills and qualifications to do the job, illuminate which areas of your experience to showcase and build interview rapport.

Bad questions, on the other hand, can drive a wedge between you and the interviewer; for example, a candidate asked an IBM recruiter shortly after the interview began, "What does IBM stand for?" The question essentially ended the interview. Had the candidate really wanted to know what IBM stood for, she should have found out on her own. Not only was it a foolish question, it also revealed to the interviewer that she was unwilling to do even a minimal amount of research. (For a detailed discussion of good interview questions, see Chapter 9.)

Hear Everyone Out

Interviewees who feel defensive and insecure have trouble listening objectively. As a result, they're prone to miscommunication.

Says Dennis Huebschman: "I've seen some brilliant answers to questions that weren't asked."

Learning to listen openly is an invaluable interviewing tool. It helps you stay connected and, if you've done your homework properly, increases the likelihood of healthy spontaneity. While the interview is undeniably serious business, when both parties can genuinely laugh at something together, it goes a long way toward building the relationship.

When Jim Kacena was interviewing for an outplacement position with Costello, Erdlen, he vividly remembers the embarrassing moment when he lit the wrong end of his cigarette. Fortunately, he and the interviewer were able to enjoy a good laugh over his mistake and his error wasn't held against him. (He got the job offer.)

"Good interviewers recognize that a certain amount of nervousness is inevitable and they won't hold it against you," says Kacena. "It's a mistake to think that you have to be perfectly controlled."

To take advantage of those spontaneous moments requires a level of good will that's often missing from interviews—especially if either party feels suspicious, defensive, or adversarial. Learning to make good feelings mutual is part of the art and skill of interviewing. But if you insist on maintaining a defensive posture, you may do so at your own career expense.

In the movie *Mr. Saturday Night,* Buddy Young, Jr., is an aging, once-famous comedian forced to interview with a new theatrical agent when his brother-agent retires from their 50-year partnership.

The new agent, a competent and sincere young woman in her 20s, arrives at their first interview unprepared to deal with the temperamental Buddy Young, Jr. (whom she's too young to remember). Expecting to spend their initial meeting getting acquainted, the comedian's acerbic tongue kicks in at the narcissistic offense.

"Young lady," he remarks sarcastically, "I'm 40 years past 'Tell me about yourself.'" Then, he drives her from the room with a string of insults and epithets that reveal his overreaction to his perceived "fall from grace."

Only in a Hollywood script would the chastened agent return a few days later, humbly apologetic for not having recognized and appreciated the stature of her famous client. Had this been real life, Buddy Young's egotism would undoubtedly have cost him a precious opportunity to renew his career.

Whether or not you approve of the idea, likability is one of the unwritten specifications of most career opportunities. While that doesn't mean interviewees

FOR YOUR INFORMATION

INTERVIEW DON'TS:

Don't plead how much you need a job. Employers have their own troubles.
Don't cry.
Don't mumble, hedge, or bluff.
Don't brag or otherwise overestimate your capabilities.
Don't try too hard.
Don't talk too much.
Don't act inferior or superior.
Don't argue, antagonize, or intimidate the interviewer.
Don't feel that the world owes you a living, or assume that the employer owes you a job. Nobody owes you anything.
Don't criticize past or present employers.

should shortchange other interview factors, it does mean there must be a concerted effort to develop good interview communication and rapport. Learn to wear your company manners and your best face. No interviewer really wants to see your dark side, except as a way of eliminating you from the competition.

"In all fairness, I think I should tell you that quite a few people are competing for this position."

7

Body English

You can imagine how pleased a food chemist was when his number one employment choice decided to fly him in for a day of interviewing. The agenda called for the chemist to spend the morning meeting with the research and development group's hiring manager and several prospective colleagues. Then, after lunch with the hiring manager, he'd present his research to a roomful of fellow scientists. Finally, he'd wind up the day by interviewing with the head R&D honcho.

By any interview standards, this would be a stressful day. Just to survive—let alone succeed—the chemist needed to be in top physical, intellectual and emotional form. Knowing that, the candidate spent days preparing. But all his plans fell apart when the airline lost his luggage.

Consequently, it was one very apologetic and insecure professional who—wearing a pair of torn blue jeans—presented himself and his work to a host of peers and senior managers.

We'll never know how much this factor directly influenced the decision not to make him an offer. I do know that the chemist found the situation so unnerving that it was impossible for him to settle comfortably into his game plan.

Besides reminding you to carry your suit on the plane with you next time you travel to an interview, this lost luggage story should also drive home for you the relationship between appearance and performance. When you're uncomfortable with the visual image you present, your timing and presentation will be thrown off.

Controlling Your Actions

Career counselor Debra Benton, author of *Lions Don't Need to Roar* (New York: Warner Books, 1992), says: "People form their impressions of you by looking at the outside and making assumptions about what's on the inside. They take you at face value. It's your responsibility to establish that value—and establish it quickly. It can take a lot of time and effort to undo a bad first impression."

Physical appearance isn't the only ingredient in a first impression. Consider the case of a poised and well-groomed banker who took great pains to project the right image in an interview with an investment banking firm. His perfectly tailored navy pinstripe suit, white shirt and red tie and carefully coiffed black hair cut an impressive "I know how to carry myself" image. His black wire-rimmed glasses added just the right touch of smarts to his professional demeanor.

As he sat confidently waiting for the hiring manager, he opened his leather briefcase one last time to make sure everything he needed was in place. But when he realized he'd forgotten to bring his business cards and an extra copy of his resume, he lost his composure briefly. As luck would have it, the hiring manager came out at that exact moment and found the candidate swearing vehemently to himself in a loud whisper. The banker's short fuse left a lasting (negative) first impression.

Remember that you're being judged from the moment you arrive at a company. Before you ever say a word, people have made assumptions about what kind of person you are, and whether they want to know you better.

To make sure you win the audience over, strive to "be consciously aware of and conscientiously in control of your actions for at least the first four minutes of every encounter," advises Debra Benton. "Obviously, you'll want to maintain a positive presence throughout . . . but if you tune in extrasensitively and stay on

```
┌────────────────────────────────────────────────────────────┐
│                 FOR YOUR INFORMATION                         │
├────────────────────────────────────────────────────────────┤
│                                                              │
│            PUT YOUR BEST SELF FORWARD                        │
│                                                              │
│  When you interview for a job, you always carry three        │
│  people into an employer's office:                           │
│                                                              │
│  1. Who you think you are.                                   │
│  2. Who you really are.                                      │
│  3. Who others perceive you to be.                           │
│      It's up to you to project your best self.               │
│                                                              │
└────────────────────────────────────────────────────────────┘
```

top of your behavior for those first four minutes, you'll almost always [achieve] the effect you want."

The Handshake

A host of research studies have determined that 65 to 85 percent of all communication is transmitted nonverbally. And to an astute observer, your physical mannerisms provide insight into your emotional state. Hiring managers will peg you as nervous or uninterested if you're fidgety, shaky or as unresponsive as a corpse during interviews. Thus, it's important to take control of your body language from the start.

A simple handshake can work wonders (or create disaster). A few years ago, I interviewed with the director of a corporate outplacement center who literally radiated physical energy. Initially, he conveyed that vitality with a masterful handshake that still lingers in my memory.

We all know the admonishments against a "dead fish" handshake. But what is it about a person's grip that has such distinguishing power? At first, I thought it was just the strength with which the director clasped my hand. Recently, when I met (and shook hands) with him again, I realized there was more to it than that. As our palms met, I noticed that he held our hands in place for a fraction longer than normal—a subtle gesture that, in my mind, conveyed warmth. As he did so, he also simultaneously made eye contact with me and started talking about how nice it was to see me again. It would have been impossible not to feel welcome.

In that case, I experienced firsthand what it meant to be the recipient of a powerful self-presentation. On the flip side, Tom Hounihan, president of Hounihan

Associates, in Palos Hills, Illinois, remembers being advised by outplacement consultant Judy Hudson that he shook hands with women too softly.

"Basically, she told me that it would be perceived as chauvinistic," he says.

Energy Level

Interviewers also watch your eyes. When Hounihan was training director for a Chicago hospital, he remembers a candidate who (though well-credentialed) kept her eyes on the floor throughout the entire interview. "There was no spark or gleam in her eyes when she talked," Hounihan says. "It tied into the rest of her body language—which was all kind of 'slumped over.' It was obvious her self-esteem was dragging on the floor."

Understandably, employers consider your comportment in interviews a clue as to whether you can do the job and how well you'll fit into their environment.

New Orleans labor attorney Stefanie Allweiss prefers surrounding herself with extremely confident, high-energy professionals like herself. When interviewing candidates for associate positions with her firm, she's most concerned with their level of energy and enthusiasm.

"By the time candidates reach me, their basic credentials have already been established," says Allweiss. "I'm more interested in how relaxed they are. If they look like they're going to break out in welts any minute, I can't imagine how they'll handle the stress of a trial practice."

Allweiss also looks at how "interesting" candidates are. "Do they have a little life in them? Or are they totally overrehearsed? I don't want to work with a drone," she says.

Benton believes that "relaxed energy" is a crucial component of a successful professional persona. Relaxed physical energy (unlike nervous energy) conveys poise and self-confidence. For example, something as simple as the way you enter a room can announce vividly "I'm here." To facilitate that goal, Benton recommends that you pause slightly before entering the interviewer's office, determine where you want to sit, then settle in.

"You have a limited time to show people what you're made of," says Benton. "If you anxiously rush into a room and hurry to your seat, scarcely acknowledging anyone or anything in your path, slink in like a scared puppy or slip in surreptitiously so you can come and go without anyone noticing you were there, then you waste precious time."

Your Posture

Posture is another key to conveying physical energy. A psychologist who was used to listening to her patients in a somewhat reclining posture unconsciously transferred that behavior to the interview setting. A videotaped "mock interview" tipped her off that what she intended to be an expression of relaxed involvement actually looked more like slouching. By sitting up straight and leaning toward the interviewer, she created a more favorable impression of herself as an active listener.

A salesperson who was used to making public presentations had a similarly disconcerting experience when he viewed himself on videotape. His rude awakening came from watching his own nervous habits. He found his constant fiddling with his hair and tie "very distracting."

Taking Notes

One way to siphon your physical nervousness into intellectual energy is by taking notes. This approach gives you something useful to do with your hands and also can create the sense of a calmer, more involved listener.

But like any tool, it can be misused or misunderstood. So before dragging out pen and paper, observe a few basic rules: First, be sure you ask the interviewer's permission (some employers find it disconcerting). Second, don't get so involved in taking notes that you lose touch with the interviewer. (Make periodic eye contact and nod your head occasionally to show you're receiving the interviewer's message.) Finally, use your notes productively to organize your thoughts and questions and to provide feedback to the employer.

However, if you find that note taking is strictly a defensive maneuver that keeps you from participating in the interview conversation, you'll have to abandon it for more fruitful movement.

Gestures

Hand Gestures

Hand gestures provide another good outlet for nervous energy. A corporate attorney interviewing for a new general counsel position likes to describe how he developed a state-of-the-art statistical package to analyze business holdings. To keep the story from getting too dry, he illustrates it by sketching a picture of a bell curve in the space between himself and the interviewer.

A corporate psychologist uses a similar approach when describing a career decision-making process. She draws a quick matrix in the air with her hand, then shows how interests are charted on the horizontal axis and abilities on the vertical axis. "It helps people picture it," she says.

While hand gestures are great for illustrating concepts and displaying intellectual vigor, they can also demonstrate pure emotional energy. A brand manager was asked whether he felt his marketing efforts were successful. The "thumbs-up" sign he flashed the interviewer said more than words.

It takes a certain emotional comfort with yourself (and your role) to use your physicality effectively. When you feel insecure or uncertain, you may miss out on good opportunities to do so.

Remember the actuary described in Chapter 6, who lost out on a professional opportunity because he was perceived as too intense? Imagine his chagrin when a very casual hiring manager (at a different company) bounced into the room, slouched down in his chair and said "Shoot!" The astonished candidate's first impulse was to point his index fingers like a six-gun and say "Bang! Bang!" Remembering professional decor, however, he stifled the urge.

Too bad. Had he done so, he probably would have established a friendlier context for the rest of the conversation.

Facial Gestures

You can also build (or erase) emotional credibility through facial gestures. When asked about his relationship with his current boss, an operations manager allowed his expression to undo his words. The candidate *said* he'd gained broad-based experience as a result of his boss' diverse personal projects. However, his quizzical half-smile told a different story.

Likewise, a former marketing manager's spontaneous grimace at the mention of her former employer blotted out the studied neutrality of her words.

Sometimes, neutral words are the best you can manage. In such cases, make sure your demeanor doesn't give your hand away. "When you say one thing and do another, it makes you look phony," Hounihan says. "Actions always speak louder than words."

Body language communicates on a two-way street. Interviewers send out their own set of nonverbal communications. While it's important to read these cues and respond accordingly, many candidates let their insecurities skew their perceptions. This can lead to some unfortunate misunderstandings.

Don't imagine a hidden meaning in every gesture. If an interviewer rubs her nose while you're speaking, she may just have an itchy nose.

Or, as Freud liked to say, "Sometimes a cigar is just a cigar."

If you feel relatively sure that you're getting negative feedback, you probably should check it out. Just don't assume you know what the interviewer is thinking and feeling; you're likely to misread the situation. Instead, ask directly what the "offending" reaction means.

A candidate felt very unsettled by an interviewer who kept trying to stifle yawns. Finally, she asked him outright: "Am I off target? Would you like me to focus on something else?"

"You're fine," the interviewer responded. "It's my kids who aren't. They have the flu and I was up all night taking care of them."

Gestures That Relay Hidden Messages

Sometimes, oversensitivity to perceived male chauvinism can interfere with the development of a productive relationship. A CFO who stands by his chair until the women in the room are seated is considered by some women "sexist." It helps if a woman can take (and appreciate) the gesture the way it was intended, as a sign of respect and politeness. (One woman candidate likes to reciprocate by helping men on with their coats to show courtesy and respect.)

Other gestures express more overt sexual motivation. An office manager remembers interviewing with a law firm whose flirtatious senior partner winked at her in the midst of the meeting. Since she knew she wouldn't be working directly for him, she chose not to let it bother her. (After being hired, she wasn't surprised to find that the partner carried on in exactly the same way with all female employees.) Other women would have been more outraged. For them, this position would not have been a match.

Your strongest reactions may take place when the other person is talking. A common job-hunter peeve is interviewers who spend all their time talking about themselves. When an interviewer endlessly pontificates, you may find yourself getting intensely bored. Rather than yawning, getting that glazed-over look or searching around the room for something more interesting to focus on, you have to find a way to get back in the game.

Nod. Smile. Take notes. Look for interesting ways to intervene without offending.

One interviewee likes to place her index finger vertically across her lips and nose as if she's saying "Shhhh." In fact, it's her way of preventing herself from interrupting the interviewer. But occasionally it's had an interesting effect on others (who thought the gesture was meant for them).

During other (more engrossing) discussions, she has a habit of cupping her chin in her hand thoughtfully, in a way that's slightly reminiscent of Rodin's "Thinker." In these moments, she conveys the impression (without ever saying a word) that she's a responsive and contemplative person.

People read our feelings through our body gestures. So, it's crucial that we take responsibility for the messages we send. Says Debra Benton: "It's a great opportunity to live the kind of employee you're going to be."

"Aha! A clip-on tie! I'm afraid that knocks $5,000 off of your starting salary!"

8

Dealing with the Unexpected

Uninitiated job hunters usually expect to meet directly with the hiring manager. And if the interview goes well, they expect to receive a job offer at the end of the conversation. Anything less proves disappointing.

But this is seldom the way employers work. Instead of setting yourself up for disappointment, learn to manage your anxiety (and expectations) through insight and preparation.

The following sections provide a closer look at some of the structural deviations employers build into the interviewing process.

Screening Interviews

These interviews can take place on the telephone or in person, and are usually conducted by a human resources (HR) professional or executive recruiter. Their goal is to determine whether you have the minimum qualifications for the position. Your goal is to stop them from weeding you out and win a face-to-face meeting.

How do you accomplish that?

The rules remain the same: Establish rapport, and sell your qualifications. In telephone interviews, however, you have an additional obstacle. Because you never know when an interviewer will call, it's easy to get caught off guard.

Situation: You're just about to sit down to dinner with your family. The kids are roughhousing in the living room, and the television is blaring. The phone rings—it's an HR person saying he's received your resume and would like to ask you a few questions. What do you do?

"Buy some time to get ready," advises Tom Washington. Patricia Berg agrees that you shouldn't feel compelled to conduct an interview on the spot. "If you're in the midst of something else, you'll never come across well," she says.

You can regain control of the situation by using a rapport builder, such as "We just sat down to dinner. Let me move to my office and call you back in 15 minutes." Fifteen minutes may not seem like a long time, but if you're organized, it's long enough to review your notes, prepare your major selling points and calm your nerves.

A recruiter remembers calling a candidate about an office manager position. First, the candidate asked, "What job is this?"

The recruiter answered, then there was a minute or two of paper rustling. Finally, the candidate got back on the phone and asked, "Can you read my letter back to me?"

The recruiter replied, "No. Goodbye."

Telephone interviews can also be a test of how you handle yourself. A computer programmer remembers receiving a call from a Hewlett-Packard recruiter at 2 A.M. Since the job required a lot of on-call experience, we can safely assume that this was a test of the candidate's responsiveness. It also says a lot about the company and the position.

In this latter example, we can safely assume that (if hired) this candidate would have lots of on-call responsibilities.

Candidates who understand the meaning of an employer's actions during the interview process will undoubtedly want to ask some questions of their own about the employer's expectations for the position.

Some initial screening interviews take place in person with a company's HR representative. When you're called to set up an appointment, avoid the impulse to schedule your meeting immediately. You're better off having some time to do your homework than being the first (unprepared) candidate who walks in the door. Ask the recruiter for company brochures and a job description to help you get ready.

HR interviews typically follow a structured question-answer format that revolves around technical qualifications. Your main task is to prove you have those qualifications. However, that doesn't mean you should neglect the rapport-building possibilities in the situation. You never know how much influence HR will play in the hiring decision, and having the screener pass along your resume with some glowing comments certainly can't hurt. An enthusiastic recommendation is obviously better than a lukewarm one.

Videotape interviews are another screening device. They're usually conducted by an outside service or recruiter who's trying to handle multiple interviews quickly. This format leaves no room for rapport building. Mostly, it's an on-camera performance in which you recite your credentials (or read your resume) to a stone-faced interviewer. Unless you're a real camera-ham, this can be very disconcerting.

Remember to keep your answers short and objective, look at the camera when you speak—and try to look happy about the whole adventure.

Sequential Interviews

Many companies hire by consensus. As a result, you may find yourself meeting with multiple hiring authorities.

One candidate for a management position with a Milwaukee bank was asked to meet with 12 different people in one day. This proved to be an unmanageable task. He knocked himself out of the running when interviewer 9 asked him what he thought of interviewer 7. When the candidate half-criticized interviewer 7's approach, interviewer 9 commented, "Too bad you didn't like her. She's my protégée."

To avoid such disasters, treat each interview as "new and fresh." Ask questions and try to build a relationship with every individual you meet. That will enhance the spontaneity of the event, and you won't feel so much like a robot or someone's repetitious pet parrot. Also, consider the process a chance to improve your interview skills; what better way to get your spiel down cold than by practicing it a dozen times in one day.

Group Interviews

A candidate for a bank management position was interviewed by two Japanese managers. After each of his answers, the two interviewers conversed earnestly with each other in Japanese.

This scenario is enough to make even the most secure candidate wince. Rather than sit there uncomfortably (as he did), the candidate might have taken more control over the situation by asking the managers, "Did you need some clarification of my answer?"

In the meantime, he learned a lot about the culture of the firm. Accepting a position with this bank would inevitably mean feeling left out of many conversations.

Group and panel interviews are intimidating simply because of the sheer number of people involved. As the outsider, you can easily feel overwhelmed by the barrage of questions. In such situations, it's often helpful to use a technique salespeople rely on to get committees to decide in their favor. Monica Tulley did this when she interviewed for a corporate strategic planning job. During the meeting, she asked each panel member what he or she wanted from the position and tried to get a consensus of opinion. Eventually, she got them to agree that they wanted a set of five-year goals and, in the process, convinced them she could do the job.

However, you need excellent group facilitation skills—and the right group—to succeed with this approach. A Chicago-area meeting planner was asked to interview with the 12-member executive committee of a nonprofit association. During the meeting, there were so many competing agendas (including disagreement over whether the position should even exist) that the candidate realized that until the group could agree more, the job was undoable.

In another case, a vocational counselor interviewed with an entire mental-health team for a newly created position. She spent most of her time educating department members about the role of vocational counseling in a mental health clinic, making it less like a job interview and more like an educational seminar.

There are endless variations on the theme.

A law office manager candidate was invited to a half-day round-robin interview with more than 30 attorneys. She was seated at the head of a long conference table with a dozen attorneys staring down at her. They started asking the standard questions: "Tell us about yourself." "Why do you want to work here?" "Why are you leaving your current job?" and so on. Periodically, one or two attorneys would get up and leave—soon to be replaced by other members of the firm. When the new interviewers began asking questions she'd already answered, the first group got up and left—while the candidate had to plunge into her explanation once more.

Consensus building was obviously not an option under these circumstances. Indeed, the Grand Inquisition was so intimidating that this candidate had her hands full just fielding questions and trying to make eye contact with questioners. Had she been more savvy, she would've tried to slow the process down by interacting with each interviewer more closely.

Then, there was the woman who was interviewed by 45 people all at once. Her interview felt more like a press conference.

Why do employers choose these formats? Obviously, it's an expedient way to have everyone meet the candidate at once. It also gives decision makers the luxury of safety in numbers. But it's undoubtedly harder on the candidate.

Stress Interviews

While all interviews are, by definition, stressful, stress interviews are designed to test your reactions to specific situations. The theory is that you'll reveal in the interview how you'll actually handle stress when it occurs on the job.

A candidate who interviewed with a stock brokerage firm was put in a room for 90 minutes with a phone, notepad, list of names and instructions to sell stocks. On the other end were people the company had arranged to give him a hard time.

In some cases, though, the stress applied seems so artificial that it's difficult to gauge exactly what employers learn from the experiment. Before so many offices became smoke-free, many employers were known to offer candidates cigarettes without supplying ashtrays. (Apparently, the test was whether you asked for an ashtray, flicked your ashes in the cuff of your pants or squashed your cigarette out on the butt of your hand.)

A method used more frequently now is asking rapid-fire questions that barely give the interviewee a chance to think.

Richard Silverman, president of a St. Louis-based management consulting firm that bears his name, says "When barraged with questions from all directions, a candidate should feel free to slow things down." For example, you might turn to one interviewer and say, "You ask a very important question that I'd be delighted to answer, Mr. Jones. But before I address that issue, I need to finish responding to Ms. Smith's question."

Another common stress test involves the use of silence. A manager of a pharmaceutical company liked to throw candidates off balance by beginning the interviews with silence—for as long as necessary. For him, the way candidates broke the silence was a test of their relationship skills. Since the job involved crisis intervention on a telephone helpline, he felt it was important to see how candidates would react in the absence of a verbal response.

In this situation, candidates have three good options, all of which involve taking control:

1. Ask permission to begin the interview—"Would you like me to begin?"

2. Start the interview in the absence of a question—"Let me tell you a little about myself."

3. Ask a question about the organization—"Can you give me more information about the position?"

Another stress test involves asking weird questions to determine how the interviewee responds. An assessment specialist with an engineering firm likes to use "If you could be any animal, what would it be?" as a psychological teaser. When faced with such questions, you have several alternatives:

1. Answer the question and let the interviewer interpret the data (without any further input from you).

2. Answer the question, then ask for feedback—"I think I'd like to be a porpoise. What does that mean to you?"

3. Answer the question and give your own interpretation—"I'd like to be a dolphin because dolphins are graceful and highly intelligent."

4. Answer the question with a question—"Can you tell me how this relates to the position?"

Whenever you're faced with a stress interview, the first step is to recognize that you're in the situation. Once you realize what's happening, it's much easier to stay calm because you can mentally reframe the situation. Then you have two choices: Play along or refuse to be treated so poorly.

"Follow your instincts," says Pat Berg. "Do what you'd do in other similar situations."

One caveat: If you do decide to play along, make sure you find out later why the interviewer chose to use a stress interview. This will tell you a great deal about the company and the position. If there's a legitimate reason, you may still want to work there. But if they're just sadistic people on a power trip, you should know that, too.

Performance Interviews

As part of the interview process, you may be asked to showcase your skills.

When Ruben Lamarque, a former sales manager with AT&T, made a transition into college teaching, one school asked him to present a portion of a business course to colleagues. In that presentation, he needed to demonstrate platform skills and a knowledge of his subject material.

Ditto for Lana Steinman, an experienced sales trainer who expected—and was routinely asked—to teach a segment of a training program as part of her evaluation process.

Fortunately, both Lamarque and Steinman are polished presenters unlikely to suffer from performance anxiety. But not every candidate shares their love of the podium. When your livelihood is hanging in the balance, I know lots of candidates who would gladly pass on the public speaking challenge.

Like it or not, however, there are some types of jobs where candidates are routinely expected to make group presentations. In the world of research and development, for example, there is a well-established precedent that scientists present the results of their research to their professional colleagues. This protocol has been known to strike terror into the hearts of research professionals, many of whom feel more comfortable in the laboratory than at the lectern.

While interviewing for a position as the administrative director of a sleep disorder clinic, a research psychologist was asked to present the results of his research to the employer's management team.

He channeled his anxiety into the preparation, working long hours to write a well-organized paper and create audiovisuals and flip charts that would clearly illustrate his points.

The goal of his extensive preparation was twofold: first, to create the impression of a thorough and well-organized professional, and second (but equally important), to leave little room for error.

True to his strengths, his performance relied more on his intellect than his personality, which he knew to be something less than dynamic.

A psychiatric social worker who was interviewing with an in-patient psychiatric hospital didn't enjoy the same luxury of time and control. When she was asked to lead a group of psychotic patients to demonstrate her skill in working with that particular population, she knew that the situation was likely to be volatile and unpredictable.

To prepare herself, she did some behind-the-scenes networking with an acquaintance who had formerly worked at the same hospital. He was able to provide her with some useful insight into both the patient population and the professional staff's preferred modus operandi.

When aptitude testing is used as a performance measure, it may be more difficult to prepare yourself except, perhaps, to brush up on some of the basic skills in your area.

Testing

Testing often serves as a tool to measure compatibility factors. Most tests are administered in a face-to-face meeting with a psychologist who interprets the results and submits a report to the hiring manager for review.

Some candidates really take offense at psychological testing. If so, you always have the right to terminate the interview; but, if you want to work for a company that subscribes to psychological testing, you'll have to bite the bullet and comply. Otherwise, you'll be screened out.

But you do have choices about how you handle your side of the testing equation. Employment professionals divide up on the issue of whether to "be yourself" or "take control." Those who fall into the latter camp recommend that candidates skew their answers to what they think the employer wants to hear.

Testing guru Ed Goedert says it's a mistake to try to psych out the assessment instruments.

"The true purpose of a psychological test is to determine whether the position and organization are a good match," says Goedert. "If it's a mistake, you need to know that, too."

But these are hard employment times, and some candidates are more concerned with getting *a job* than getting the right job. Those candidates will probably be more inclined to follow the advice of careers columnist Joyce Lain Kennedy. In *Electronic Job Search Revolution* (Wiley, 1994), she and co-author Thomas J.

Morrow suggest that job hunters prepare for personality tests by scripting out a personality statement in advance of the interview:

"Declare who you think you are. Include your characteristics. List your strengths as they apply to the job you hope to land. Write as though you were describing a character in a film script."

Others go one step further. They approach personality tests by creating a mental picture of a successful friend in a similar career field. When responding to questions, they think how that person would respond.

In keeping with that line of thinking, *Knock 'em Dead* author Martin Yate (Bob Adams Inc., 1994) recommends the following guidelines to "beat the psychological tests."

1. Never answer a question from the viewpoint of your innermost beliefs. Instead, ask yourself, "How has my experience as a professional taught me to think and respond to this?"

2. Look at yourself from the employer's point of view. Then highlight those traits the employer is most likely to value.

3. Think of people you've known who have failed on the job. What can you learn from their mistakes and make a part of the "professional you"?

4. Think of people you've known who have succeeded on the job. What have you learned from their success? How can you make this knowledge a part of the professional you?

It may not be as easy to outsmart the tests as some people think.

"It's actually much easier to fool an interviewer than a test," says Dr. Sandy Marcus, a principal with the Chicago-based testing firm of Friedland and Marcus. "Many tests have consistency factors built into them which make it difficult for applicants to fake a whole pattern of responses without getting tripped up."

Even if you do manage to fool the testing folks and get hired, you may be setting yourself up for failure. Unless you are prepared to think and act like the character you impersonated, employers may be disappointed to discover that you aren't the person you pretended to be in the interview.

Don't misunderstand me here. I'm not suggesting that you reveal every wart or turn your test-taking experience into an opportunity for true confessions. As Sandy Marcus says: "There are 1,000 different ways to represent the same truth."

Obviously, you'll want to select one that best represents you. In testing terms, that means always responding in ways that are consistent with the best you can be. That way, if and when you're hired, all you really need to do is live up to your potential.

Computer-Assisted Interviews

For some employers, computers are changing the face of their selection process.

During a typical computer-assisted interview, you sit at a terminal (or, in some cases, program information into the computer via a touch tone telephone), and work through a series of 50 to 100 multiple choice questions relating to your employment history, background and qualifications.

If you're in control of your storyline and presentation, these interviews should pose no special problem. In fact, it may be much easier to type your answers into the computer without the distraction of another person in the room.

Ironically, some candidates may get a little too comfortable for their own good.

"A lot of people are more honest with a computer than they are with interviewers," says Pat Engler-Parish, a vice president of Aspen Software in Laramie, Wyoming, developers of the Greentree Computer-Assisted Employment Interview. "In the absence of non-verbal cues, they aren't trying to please the interviewer and are more likely to tell the truth."

By way of example, Engler-Parish says she was surprised by how many candidates responded "Yes" to the question: "Have you ever stolen property?"; but she was even more astonished by the number of people who said "Yes" to the follow-up question: "Will you steal property from this company if you're hired?" And when asked "How much will you steal?", they were more than willing to be specific.

For the most part, computer-assisted interviews are designed to collect data, organize information and help employers develop probing questions around areas of concern. They aren't intended to replace the human encounter or screen out applicants (although some candidates do, in fact, get screened out during the preliminaries).

Too much candor is one clear faux pas. Overselling is another. At Aspen, the experts have a name for this phenomenon: overresponders. Sandy Marcus describes them as "self-enhancers."

Candidates who oversell themselves may lose credibility in the eyes of the employer. "If they look too good to be true," say Engler-Parish, "they probably are."

Mealtime Interviews

When dining and interviewing are combined, a number of considerations arise. Group privacy is an important issue. If the restaurant is crowded or the tables are too closely packed, you may find it difficult to speak freely. Don't be afraid to raise that concern; most interviewers will thank you for it.

Your personal privacy is also at risk. A mealtime interview can have a whole different feel to it. Because it's often a "getting-to-know-you" experience, expect lots of social questions about your car, home, kids, and so on. It's a great time to ask all those off-limits questions that would be considered illegal under other circumstances.

The challenge is in making your conversational contribution without falling into the trap of overfamiliarity. Discussions about politics, religion and other loaded subjects are still off limits. So are true confessions. The interviewer isn't your best friend (or best-friend-to-be), so don't reveal any personal or emotional problems. The employer doesn't need to know that you're getting divorced, are a recovering alcoholic or that your kids have drug problems.

Your social graces are also on display, so watch your table manners. One interviewer pays close attention to when candidates salt their food. Those who reach for the shaker without tasting first are perceived as people who may make changes hastily.

FOR YOUR INFORMATION

MIND YOUR MANNERS AT MEALTIME INTERVIEWS

1. Keep drinking to a minimum. Better yet, don't drink at all.
2. No smoking, please—unless the interviewer smokes first or you're interviewing with a tobacco company.
3. Order something easy to eat. If you're struggling with spaghetti, you won't be able to concentrate on the interview.
4. Don't overorder or choose the most expensive item on the menu. Take your cues from the interviewer.
5. Use your best manners. Don't shovel your food, talk with your mouth full or eat with your hands (unless it's finger food).

Nancy Schellhouse, the CEO of Cincinnati-based Promark Company/ Outplacement International, tells a story of a man who lost out on a CFO position when he failed an unexpected test.

When the bill came, the interviewer discovered he'd "forgotten" his wallet and asked the candidate to pay. The would-be CFO said, "No problem" and paid the bill without looking at it. Not surprisingly, the interviewer decided he didn't want a CFO who'd pay bills without looking them over first.

Out-of-Town Interviews

Out-of-town interviews involve lots of logistic concerns. Nancy Schellhouse recommends conducting a mental run-through of the whole episode to anticipate obstacles. For example, say you're flying and the plane gets grounded. What do you do? (Fly in the night before.) The airline loses your luggage. What do you do? (Carry your interview suit with you on the plane.) You don't know the city and are worried about getting lost. (Take a cab.) You're worried you won't have enough money. (Confirm that the company will be paying expenses, and carry a credit card.)

Most important, control what you can control—and hope interviewers pitch in to make your life in their city a little easier.

"I suppose you're wondering, 'Why such a low starting salary?'"

9

Your Turn to Ask

Interviewing is a two-way street. The questions you ask (and how you ask them) do as much to differentiate you from the competition as the ones you answer.

While it's important for your questions to occur spontaneously and appropriately in each specific interview conversation, it always helps to think through—and plan out—some questions ahead of time.

All-Purpose Questions

Certain questions are suitable during almost any interview. For example, no matter how thorough the interviewer's explanation of the available opening, you'll

FOR YOUR INFORMATION

THE VALUE OF QUESTIONING

Questions serve three functions for the job candidate:

1. To help you assess whether you really want the job.
2. To help you understand what the employer needs.
3. To build a working relationship grounded in give-and-take communication.

undoubtedly long for more information about job responsibilities, performance measurements, management style, organizational culture and resources. While the following list of questions isn't all-inclusive, it should provide some ideas to get you started:

1. What are the major responsibilities of this position?

2. Is there a job description? May I see it?

3. Can you tell me why this position is open?

4. How often has it been filled in the past 5 to 10 years?

5. What did you like most about the person who previously held this position?

6. What would you like to see the person who fills this position do differently?

7. What qualifications would you expect the successful candidate to possess?

8. What do you see as my strengths/weaknesses for this position?

9. What are the greatest challenges facing the person in this position?

10. What are your immediate goals and priorities for this position?

11. What kind of support does this position receive in terms of people and finances?

12. How much freedom would I have to determine my work objectives and deadlines?

13. How would my performance be measured and how is successful performance usually rewarded?

14. What career progression do you see for someone in this position? Do you normally promote from within?

15. How would you describe your management style?

16. Can you describe your organizational culture?

17. Do you have a lot of turnover? (Why or why not?)

18. How many people would I be supervising? How long have they been with the company, and what are their backgrounds?

19. Why are you looking at external candidates for this position, instead of promoting from within?

20. What do people seem to like most/least about working here?

21. Would it be possible to meet the people who work in the department?

22. Do you encourage participation in community or professional activities?

23. Do you have a management development or internal training program?

24. What are the company's plans for growth in the next five years?

25. How does the company intend to remain competitive?

Your questions must be asked in a spirit of honest and open inquiry. Tone of voice matters. For example, when asking "Why is this position open?" you can convey suspiciousness or curiosity simply by changing the inflection of your voice.

Employers have weak spots, too, and sometimes seemingly innocuous questions draw blood. I remember interviewing with an outplacement firm president who was looking to replace one of her consultants. Knowing that the consultant had moved over to a competing agency, I remarked, "I heard your consultant jumped ship to the enemy."

Unfortunately, I exposed a sensitive issue. My comment unleashed a long-winded, defensive explanation of the consultant's reasons for leaving that made it clear their parting of the ways had not been harmonious. After that, my task was to tactfully reestablish the rapport between us that my offhand comment threatened to annihilate.

Consider Your Values

Once you've covered the basics, it's important to ask about the concerns closest to your heart. After all, everyone works for the money, but money probably isn't your sole career motivator. Edgar Schein, a management professor at MIT's Sloan School of Management, developed the concept of "career anchors" to address the internal side of career development.

"The career anchor is that one element in a person's self-concept that he or she will not give up, even in the face of difficult choices," says Schein. By understanding your career anchor (what really matters most to you), you can develop a question strategy that will reveal the information you need to make a good career decision.

Unfortunately, many people believe that having a "good job" (as opposed to having just any job) is a luxury they can't afford. In reality, it's a necessity you shouldn't try to do without. "Even in a terrible economy, you have choices," says Patricia Berg. "If it's a bad match, you'll be looking again in six months or a year—with another obstacle to overcome."

In other words, kid yourself now about what really matters to you and you'll probably have to play catch-up later.

Schein's research into managerial careers identifies eight typical anchors. While I recommend that you take the inventory in Schein's book *Career Anchors* (Pensacola, FL: Pfeiffer, 1993) to determine your personal career anchor more definitively, the descriptions and suggested questions that follow should get you started thinking in the right direction.

Technical/Functional Competence

If you have a technical/functional competence career anchor, you refuse to give up the opportunity to continually develop and refine your skills. Because you derive your professional identity from the exercise of these skills, you may need to resist pressure to get kicked upstairs into a more general management role.

In addition to the general questions outlined in the beginning of this chapter, people with this anchor need to ask specific questions about the company's values. For example:

1. Would you describe your organization as a sales-, marketing-, finance- or engineering-driven firm?

2. Where does this position typically lead?

3. Do you have a technical ladder?

4. How do you encourage professional growth? (Don't ask specifically about tuition reimbursement; save discussions of employee benefits for salary negotiations).

5. Do you have a training program?

6. How do you feel about employee participation in professional activities?

7. Is there a budget to attend professional conferences?

8. What kind of support does the company provide for research?

The answers to these questions matter. Should you discover that the company doesn't have a formal technical ladder or promote the career path you hope to follow, you may decide to keep on looking for a better match.

However, you might also try exploring the possibility of creating what you want. For example, an R&D scientist with an MBA wanted to move into product development, but the company he was interviewing with had never supported this career path before. To determine the feasibility of this plan, he asked, "Would you support a career path that would help me move into the product development areas?" The company agreed to keep his career goals in mind.

General Managerial Competence

If you have a general managerial competence, you won't give up the opportunity to climb the traditional career ladder. You probably want to make a contribution at the macro level and consider specialized functions to be either a trap or mere stepping-stones to larger opportunities.

If you fall into this category, you're more likely to tie your success to organizational success. It will be important for you to establish yourself in a function central to the company's vision of its future. Essential questions for you might include:

1. How long has this position existed in your organization?

2. Does the company foresee any growth for this department?

3. What level of support is available to accomplish the department's goals?

4. Where does this position typically lead?

5. How will my performance be measured?

6. How will successful performance be rewarded?

7. How do other executives view this department/position?

Autonomy/Independence

People with an autonomy/independence career anchor need to define their work their own way. They may need flexible working conditions and hours and often welcome incentive-based pay. If this sounds like you, focus your questions on the company's management style and philosophy as well as on specific reporting relationships:

1. Who does this position report to?

2. How would you describe that executive's supervisory style?

3. What kind of appraisal system do you use to measure performance in this position?

4. Is your company environment formal or informal?

5. Do you operate in a centralized or decentralized manner?

6. How much freedom would I have to set my own goals and deadlines?

Security/Stability

If your career anchor is security/stability, you won't sacrifice employment security unless forced to. You tend to be more concerned with a job's context than its content (where you work, not what you do), and are happiest in a promotion system that rewards loyalty, seniority and dependability. Civil service or government jobs, large corporations and tenured academic positions are traditional employment homes for people with this career anchor.

Unfortunately, economic changes have made this a more difficult career anchor to achieve. Even civil service jobs aren't as stable as they once were. Many U.S. Postal Service employees were upset when the agency recently went through a major reorganization. Displaced employees were overwhelmingly committed to remaining within the system. Many accepted job transfers into other cities or unrelated positions just to stick with their employer.

To find a stable organization in this volatile employment environment, ask the following questions:

1. How would you describe the culture of your organization?

2. How stable has your organization been?

3. Has there been much turnover in this department? Why has it occurred?

4. Why is this position open?

5. Can you give me a history of this position? How often has it been filled in the past 5 to 10 years?

Entrepreneurial Creativity

People with this career anchor have an overriding need to create new products or services. Because they're motivated by an "I-can-do-it" attitude, they do well with new products and services and with start-up ventures.

A writer with a prestigious Chicago advertising firm who fit this profile was up for a promotion to creative director of a Midwest branch office. During the interview, he impressed the CEO, but he also began to question whether the organizational culture really was conducive to creativity. For example, he discovered that employees weren't allowed to personalize their cubicles with artwork or photographs. Beards and mustaches were taboo. Self-expression didn't seem to be tolerated, let alone valued. Since part of the job involved the recruitment and development of creative personnel, the writer felt the office atmosphere would make it difficult for him to recruit the kinds of talent he needed. So, despite the six-figure income he was offered, he turned the job down.

Some possible questions for entrepreneurial creative types:

1. Can you describe your organizational culture and management philosophy?

2. Do you encourage creativity?

3. Can you give me some examples of the way that the company rewards creativity?

4. Whom would I supervise in this position, and what are their backgrounds?

5. Whom would I report to, and can you tell me something about his or her background?

6. What are the most immediate challenges facing this company?

Sense of Service/Dedication to a Cause

If you're in this category, money isn't as central to you as the desire to make a contribution. Since you really want your work to make a difference, you may tie your career happiness to the organization's mission and values. Some questions you might ask:

1. What is your organizational mission?

2. How do you hope to accomplish it?

3. How does this position fit into the organization's mission?

4. What kind of qualifications do you typically look for in this position? company?

5. What do people like most/least about working here?

Pure Challenge

If you fit in this group, you want to solve seemingly insoluble problems, win out over tough competitors and overcome difficult obstacles. Think of daredevil Evel Knievel, whose career only had meaning in challenge. Some of the greatest competitors in the world fall into this category.

Some important questions:

1. What are some of the most difficult problems I'd face in this position?

2. How much manpower and financial resources will I have available to meet those challenges?

3. How committed is the organization to solving these problems?

4. Does the corporate culture encourage risk taking?

5. Can you give me some examples of a time when risk taking was rewarded?

6. How much freedom will I have to do things my own way?

Lifestyle

People with lifestyle anchors seek integration and balance. They may be most concerned with a company's attitude toward family and community responsibilities. Many of their questions center around issues of time, resources and expectations:

1. How many hours per week would a person in this position typically expect to work?

2. Can you estimate the amount of travel required?

3. Do you have company picnics? Softball teams? Christmas parties?

4. What challenges will the person in this position face in the short term? long term?

5. Are there enough resources to accomplish those objectives?

6. Do you encourage community activities?

FOR YOUR INFORMATION

WHAT ARE YOUR PRIORITIES?

Lifestyle issues are a priority for many executives. In fact, "family issues" is the number one reason cited by managers for turning down a job offer in a new location, says Dwight Foster, executive managing director for D. E. Foster & Partners, a New York search firm. Bill Walters, executive vice president of Milwaukee-based Barnes, Walter & Associates, estimates that four out of six finalists drop out of contention because they don't want to move. Family issues are the primary factor behind the refusals, he says, followed by the preference to avoid high-cost areas that erode living standards.

Learn the Employer's Wants and Needs

While it's important to use questions to determine whether a position suits your personal needs, it's also critical to explore how well you fit the company's requirements. Unless you understand what the employer needs, and demonstrate your commitment and ability to do the job, you won't get an offer.

Many questions can serve double (or even triple) duty in this regard. Nevertheless, you should develop a line of questions that focus specifically on learning the employer's wants and needs. That way, you can "sell" those skills and areas of experience that will be most impressive.

Feedback questions usually work well because they allow you to probe how the employer feels about you. Follow up a question such as "What skills and qualifications are you looking for in this position?" with "What do you see as my strengths and weaknesses for this position?"

Once you know more about the employer's specific concerns about you, you can develop a strategy to deal with them. (For an in-depth discussion of how to best deal with resistance, see Chapter 4.)

Another feedback strategy is to follow up your response to an employer's question with "Does that make sense to you?" "How do you feel about what I just said?" or "How would you like someone in this position to handle that situation?"

This tactic has the added benefit of helping you build rapport with the interviewer. Through such open give-and-take communication, you demonstrate your commitment to solving the employer's problems and plant the seeds for a good working relationship.

Similarly, questions such as "What would you like me to accomplish in this position?" help promote a "we" conclusion. This makes your desire to help clear and sends the employer a strong signal that you like what you hear and want to join the team.

Thoughtful questions also indicate to prospective employers that you've done your homework and learned as much as possible about them, says Candy Gilmore, at The H.S. Group. However, don't go overboard and turn the interview into a trivia contest.

FOR YOUR INFORMATION

A QUESTION OF CONTROL

You can steer the conversation in an interview by asking the right questions. Each time you answer a question, regain control by asking the employer one of your own. If you are asked to describe your skills, you could follow your answer by asking, "What kind of skills are you looking for?"

Mark Satterfield, formerly a human resources director with Kraft Inc., remembers interviewing a marketing assistant for a major cheese manufacturer who wanted to know how hydroponics figured in the company's future plans. Not only wasn't Satterfield sure what hydroponics were, he had even less idea what role it played in the cheese business. Although it did turn out that a small division of the company was experimenting with growing plants in nontraditional environments, Satterfield's opinion of the candidate dwindled.

"Of all the questions he could ask about the company and the job, he chose a question notable only for its obscurity," Satterfield says. "Asking a question solely to see if you can trip the interviewer seldom wins points."

Dollars-and-cents questions also destroy rapport. Unless you're at the salary negotiation stage, you should be focusing on the question of fit. Until fit has been established, you have no bargaining power, and money statements are likely to be viewed as premature demands.

One of the worst interview sins of all, though, is to say you don't have any questions. This response shows a lack of interest in and enthusiasm for the employer. Even if the interviewer has addressed most of your concerns, there's always at least one question you can ask. Perhaps you'd like to know more about the company's hiring process and time frame, for example.

Or, you can take a more lighthearted approach and ask, "How do you like me so far?"

10

The Morning After: Follow-Up and Follow-Through

The interview is over. The job has been won or lost. There's nothing left to do but sit back and wait for Judgment Day, right?

Wrong!

Often, the interview is the beginning of the hiring process, not the end. Many employers won't even consider extending an offer until they've seen the candidate's follow-up procedure.

As an officer for Continental Bank in Chicago (and later as an administrator with DeVry Institute of Technology), Jim Kacena would only hire candidates who followed up quickly and effectively. To him, job hunters' postinterview actions indicate their level of interest, desire and commitment.

"A lack of follow-up is a sign of laziness," Kacena says, "A candidate who drops the ball after the interview probably won't follow through on work assignments, either."

Thank-You Letters

Even interviewers who take less of a hard line agree that good follow-up procedures help candidates stand out from the crowd. While working for a Chicago foundation, Phyllis Edelen knew a manager who was hiring an executive assistant. The manager acknowledged that she would have been happy with either of two finalists for the position. But by sending a thank-you letter after the interview, one candidate turned the tide decisively in her favor.

"It convinced the manager that the candidate really wanted the job," Edelen says. "She wasn't sure the other candidate was all that interested."

Unfortunately, many candidates hesitate to express interest or enthusiasm to employers for fear of looking overeager. Yet the blasé approach usually backfires, as one product manager learned the hard way.

"The hiring manager told my client that she didn't get the job because she never said she wanted it," says Cheryl Heisler, president of Lawternatives, a Chicago-based career counseling firm.

A good thank-you letter is an ideal way to make sure that you express the kind of interest and enthusiasm employers desire. But it's not enough to send a form letter. You must sound genuine and sincere, and that requires a personal touch.

Kacena recalls crafting individualized thank-you letters for each of seven partners and associates at Costello, Erdlen—a now-defunct outplacement consulting firm in Boston—after he interviewed for an associate's position there. Since all seven interviews were conducted in one day, Kacena had to scribble quick notes to himself between meetings so he could later personalize his communications.

The effort paid off. Executives at the firm offered him the job (which he accepted), explaining that they'd compared his follow-up notes and were impressed with his ability to establish a personal connection with each firm member; it made him stand head and shoulders above the other candidates.

Besides expressing interest in a position, thank-you letters can reinforce or correct a first expression, or build on the relationship you've already established

---

FOR YOUR INFORMATION

WRITE THANK-YOU LETTERS THAT SELL

A follow-up letter should be more than a polite thank-you. Crafted properly, it can be a powerful selling tool. Use the following four-part structure to get more mileage from your message:

1. Tell the interviewer how much you enjoyed meeting him or her.
2. Express your enthusiasm for the company and job.
3. Reiterate a specific selling point.
4. Establish your next point of contact.

---

with an interviewer, says Ruben Lamarque, a former sales manager with AT&T. He adds that sending quality correspondence will reflect favorably on your personality and writing style. "Personally, I'm impressed by a really creative, professional and timely acknowledgment and/or recap of the interview."

Lamarque practiced what he preaches while making a transition into college teaching after taking early retirement from AT&T. While interviewing for a position with Barat College in Lake Forest, Illinois, Lamarque met with a business school dean who prided himself on his excellent relationships with students.

Admitting that it felt a bit like apple-polishing, Lamarque penned the following in his thank-you letter to the dean: "It's obvious to me, from our brief discussion, that you must be very popular with students . . . "

Then, Lamarque described his own pride in having mentored many protégés during his corporate career, and expressed his desire to continue mentoring as a teacher. Not only did Lamarque get the job, he now tries to emulate the popular dean.

Additional Follow-Up Techniques

Responding to Special Requests

You have to have a certain people-style to get away with flattery. More guarded (or jaded) job hunters may find that this technique rings artificial for them. You must find your own style. If you feel uncomfortable openly complimenting an employer, it isn't a necessity (simply a nicety).

You might try focusing instead on some aspect of the interviewer's organization that particularly interests you or where, perhaps, you'd like to get more involved. Simply expressing a desire to learn more about a specific function or area is its own kind of compliment. A refusal to do so, however, can be equally telling.

A clinical psychologist was hoping to direct the start-up efforts of a new private psychiatric hospital in the Chicago suburbs. Since the hospital was hiring an entire clinical staff, they were looking for people with innovative ideas about how to develop and market their services.

To get a feeling for the psychologist's thinking, the hiring manager asked him to write a short proposal explaining how he might approach the question of program and service development. The psychologist refused.

"If they want my ideas, they have to pay for them," the psychologist said. "I'm not going to give them away for free."

He never got the chance. Even though he was truly interested in the position, he wasn't willing to make the effort required to receive an offer. Yet, when he didn't get the job, he was disappointed and angry.

You may sympathize with the psychologist. After all, why should he have to work so hard for an employer who may never hire him? Why should he give his expertise away for free? Or invest himself in an organization that might just steal his ideas?

Why? Because he really wanted the job. And they were really interested in him. But his refusal to substantiate his skills proved problematic for them. Not only did they remain unsure of his abilities, they questioned whether he'd be the kind of employee who would give the 110 percent effort they wanted and needed.

Overcoming Doubts

To prevent such mishaps, part of your follow-up goal should be to actively determine what reservations the employer may have about hiring you. Then, you must actively work to resolve these issues, or you won't get an offer. This process begins with an honest critique of your interview performance. Ask yourself if there's some objection that you didn't completely rectify (and what would be the best way to do so).

"Any time you feel that something is wrong, don't put your head in the sand and wish it would go away," says Cheryl Heisler. "It might make the difference between getting an offer and losing out on the opportunity."

One attorney—who was enjoying his employment sabbatical a little too much—recognized he'd need to correct a bad impression quickly if he wanted a job offer. When a recruiter from a corporate law firm had asked him when he'd be available to start, the attorney mentioned a date outrageously in the future. One look at the recruiter's dismayed face told him he'd erred. But he didn't immediately retract his statement for fear of looking too defensive.

Thinking the encounter over afterward, the lawyer realized that his answer had certainly revealed his ambivalence about going back to work so soon. Wishing to make up for the error, the lawyer telephoned the recruiter the following day.

"I realize I made a mistake," the candidate said. "I'm really excited about the position and can't wait that long to start." This call helped alleviate the recruiter's concern and allowed the firm to move forward in the hiring process.

Outplacement consultant Richard Ehlers approves of this candidate's proactive approach. "Always look for obstacles and how you can resolve them. If you sense an interviewer's reluctance, call up and say 'What else can I do to convince you?'" he advises.

If you understand (and can empathize with) an employer's reservations, you can also take some steps to overcome them. During his AT&T career, Lamarque remembers interviewing with a manager who was starting a new strategic planning and development department in Texas.

Although Lamarque was very interested in the position, he knew that his lack of experience in strategic planning was a major stumbling block. So, even before the interview, he started educating himself about the discipline by reviewing relevant literature. And he continued that process in earnest afterward. Along the way, he discovered several provocative articles on the subject that he thought the interviewing manager might not have seen.

On three separate occasions, Lamarque sent an article to the manager along with a brief (empathic) note suggesting that the information inside might help him with his task.

Although he can't be certain that these articles and notes clinched the deal, Lamarque did get a phone call from the hiring manager shortly after his second "mailgram" indicating that he was, indeed, a viable candidate. A few weeks later, he received an offer and accepted the position.

Dealing with Silence

Too often, candidates assume that silence from an employer means rejection. Usually, it just means that the employer is making the hiring decision more slowly than anticipated. Tolerating the company's pace (and your anxiety) is part of the psychological task.

But while your job search may not be the firm's first priority, that doesn't mean you have to sit around anxiously twiddling your thumbs. You can use that time constructively to build your relationship and credibility with the interviewer, and convince him or her to decide in your favor.

Consider the strategy of a sales representative with a Midwestern wholesale manufacturer. She had a very good interview with a sales promotion company, but the recruiter had said she was hesitant to hire someone without industry experience. She'd also mentioned that she was still actively looking at other candidates.

The rep took the recruiter's ambivalence seriously, but not personally. After all, overcoming objections was part of her everyday selling life. So she viewed the reservations as a challenge to change the hiring manager's mind and priorities.

The rep began by educating herself about the industry. She interviewed with the company's competitors and did her best to learn more about the marketplace. In addition to weekly check-in calls to the hiring manager, she took the initiative to attend a trade show where the company was exhibiting and stopped by the booth to say hello.

Although the hiring decision dragged on for several months, the rep kept her spirits up by actively pursuing opportunities with other employers while simultaneously building her case with the sales promotion firm. Ultimately, her efforts paid off. She was extended an offer in large part, she was told, because of her persistence and energy. She'd shown the hiring manager what a convincing and tenacious salesperson she'd be.

Some candidates might consider this rep's active pursuit of the position (in the face of obvious resistance) pesty. The experts disagree. More people lose out on jobs because they aren't aggressive enough in the follow-through, they say, than the other way around.

Says Phyllis Edelen: "Most candidates hold themselves back too much. They're afraid to look too pushy, but they end up looking too passive. In fact, aggressive follow-up is one way for candidates to separate themselves from the crowd in a positive way."

"People who don't follow up are like salesmen who don't close the deal," adds Cheryl Heisler. "Why shortchange yourself at the end?" Some candidates don't follow up assertively because of emotional or psychological conflicts. They're not good at marketing themselves because it feels too needy or self-serving to chase after employers. The whole idea of declaring their interests and desires to interviewers who might reject them is highly unpalatable. They feel the need to be more self-protective and can't (or don't) follow up because they fear rejection.

Using References Wisely

One way to work around that mental block involves using third parties who may be willing to speak to prospective employers on your behalf. For example, recommendation letters can confirm what a great employee you are. You can attach these documents to a thank-you letter, or make a special point of dropping them off at the employer's office with a statement such as "Based on our conversation about my relationship with my former supervisor, I thought you might be interested in this letter of recommendation."

For a more individualized approach, ask your supporters (former bosses, teachers, co-workers, clients) to write an individualized endorsement letter and mail it directly to the employer. That way, their comments can be tailored to your needs.

Telephone references can also build your credibility (and employers' interest). But before you supply names and phone numbers, let your references know what's happening: who will be calling, what position you're up for, and what points you'd like emphasized. By prepping your references, you reinforce your relationship with them (which undoubtedly will make them sound more spontaneously enthusiastic about you) and ensure that the information presented about you will be relevant. Consider it your chance to help them become better reference givers.

Relying on third parties can backfire, as one chagrined sales manager discovered. His boss, as a direct result of the reference check, managed to establish a rapport with the hiring manager and finesse an interview for the same position. Things like this can happen. However, if you dwell on the possibility of such disasters, you'll make yourself overly suspicious and guarded at a time when you need to be open and enthusiastic. Rather than leaping to the conclusion that you can't trust anyone, consider this story a warning to rethink your relationships with your own references. If you can't trust them, you shouldn't be using them. But if you can, then make sure you maximize their effect.

FOR YOUR INFORMATION

FOLLOW-UP WITH CONTACTS

If your interview was the result of a networking contact, part of your follow-up should include a call to your networking source. This can motivate your contact to redouble his or her efforts on your behalf, stimulate a conversation about you between the interviewer and your contact, and help you get additional information about the position and the company.

Getting the Offer

Finally, don't assume a position is wrong for you until you have all the facts. Many job hunters don't follow up after interviews because they're not sure they really want the job. Then, if they don't get an offer, the decision is out of their hands.

Ehlers believes that this is the wrong approach. "Candidates need to go after every job as if they wanted it," he says. "The goal should be to receive the offer. Then you can decide whether to accept it or not."

Pursuing all relevant job opportunities seriously should give you a more positive mental framework, he says. When you know you can get job offers, your self-esteem and candidacy will benefit. Ehlers recommends depersonalizing the process by developing effective follow-up skills. Scripting out telephone conversations and finding a partner who will role-play with you may help.

"If your goal is to receive the offer every time, then you can develop a set of follow-up procedures that come naturally," he says. "Practice your follow-up procedures until they become second nature. This will take you past the point of fear."

It might also help to rethink your attitude toward rejection. Admittedly, being turned down is painful. But it isn't the end of the world—just of a specific opportunity. What's more, an outright rejection can be beneficial if you're thick-skinned enough to pursue some feedback.

If you didn't get a position you felt you were really well-qualified for, ask why. Given the rampant fear of litigation, employers may not always be willing to tell you the truth. But when they do, the insight can be invaluable. Remember, for example, the actuary who learned that his interview style was too intense and made employers uncomfortable. After that, he always strove to inject some lightness and humor into his presentations.

Many times, the problems causing a rejection are easily remedied. When Tom Hounihan was interviewing for a job as a corporate trainer, a recruiter told him his appearance wasn't "crisp enough" for corporate America. So Hounihan started getting his shirts professionally starched and laundered, and soon after, he landed a training position with AT&T. In his case, something as simple as well-pressed clothing may have made the crucial difference.

Asking for feedback after a rejection has another benefit: It enables you to maintain a relationship with employers and encourages them to revisit their decision. (One engineer who sought feedback after receiving a rejection letter was amazed and delighted to find out that the letter was a mistake; she was still a candidate for the position.) And even if there's no immediate effect, it may pay off down the road.

Of course, pursuing feedback in the proper spirit isn't always easy. You may be furious at the way an employer treated you, or strongly disagree with the firm's employment decision. A colleague of mine (who should know better) remembers interviewing with a national outplacement consulting firm to be a managing partner. He was interviewed by a corporate psychologist who had flown in from another city. Not only did the psychologist arrive late, she spent the entire interview shoveling in her spaghetti lunch and glancing at her watch every two or three minutes. She ended the interview abruptly, saying she was late and had to make a phone call. She got up, paid the check and disappeared.

Unable to control his temper, my colleague sent a scathing follow-up note telling her how offensive and inappropriate he found her behavior. Obviously, he never heard back. And, although he says he doesn't regret his action, he realizes that he should have held his temper in check.

Such emotional eruptions are most likely to occur when your frustration level is high. Recognize those moments. Don't follow up with employers when you're frustrated with them (or your situation) and have an ax to grind. Anger and hostility are not endearing sentiments. Wait until you can speak calmly, rationally and professionally.

"It never makes sense to burn your bridges, even if you don't want to work for an employer," says Ehlers. "You never know when that will come back to haunt you."

No one denies that employers can, at times, be difficult to deal with. They want you to want them before they ever say that they want you. They can move with unbearable slowness, dragging on the hiring process for weeks and months. They can be unable to take or return your calls, but when they call you, they want you to be available yesterday. They can set up an interview process that approximates running an Olympic decathlon (complete with hurdle jumping).

Don't be overly sensitive. Your job (for now) is to make the employer want you. The best way to do that is to make a lasting impression with your energy, commitment and determination. After that, the decision is yours.

"I realize you said you'd be late for the interview, but five years is a long time, Stan."

11

The Headhunter Connection

Executive recruiters (aka "headhunters") are matchmakers who arrange meetings between hiring companies and candidates, and typically specialize in certain industries, functions and candidate levels.

Different Kinds of Recruiters

Retained recruiters operate at the most senior levels of management and usually work with executives in the $75,000+ salary range. *Contingency* recruiters usually work one notch lower, recruiting from the professional and middle-management ranks where annual salaries of $40,000 to $75,000 are more the norm. Retained and contingency recruiters are paid differently. Retained consultants receive a fee just to conduct the candidate search, whether or not it's successful, whereas contingency recruiters only get paid if (and when) they make a placement. But since both are paid by client companies, not job hunters, in the end this means their loyalty will always lie with the client—not with you.

The way recruiters are paid tends to dictate their style of working with candidates. As a retained recruiter, Joy Reed-Belt often works with her client corporations to develop "job specs." Not only is she intimately familiar with their corporate culture, she considers herself part of their team.

"My first loyalty is to my client corporation," says Reed-Belt. "The art of what I do is in finding the perfect match for their team."

Steve Xagas, a retained recruiter in the manufacturing and service sectors for a Geneva, Illinois, firm that bears his name, agrees:

"I consider myself part of a corporation's executive management team," says Xagas. "I know their politics and their personalities."

While contingency recruiters also have established relationships with client firms and know a great deal about their corporate cultures and needs, they play more of an outsider's role. Because they don't get paid unless they actually make a placement, they're usually more interested in developing a network of candidates they can market to prospective employers.

"A recruiter is only as good as his or her portfolio of candidates," says Florence Yee, a senior search consultant with A.L. Associates Inc. in New York City, who specializes in working with money managers. "So when good candidates present themselves to me, I go out of my way to build a relationship with them."

FOR YOUR INFORMATION

WATCH WHAT YOU SIGN

Most headhunters collect their fees from the company, so the service to the job seeker is free. Be sure you understand the payment obligations before you sign anything or hand over any money. Don't hook up with an agency that requires money up front before finding you a job. If you're still tempted, check the firm's reputation with your state's office of consumer protection.

According to the *Fordyce Letter,* a St. Louis-based newsletter for employment professionals published by Paul Hawkinson, some candidates are so sought after that recruiters present them widely, in hopes of drumming up additional search business. To qualify, though, they must be easily placeable—with skills, experience and accomplishments that are exceptional, in high demand and low supply.

For example, a senior loan officer who was relocating to a major Southwestern city had such strong credentials that two different recruiters marketed her heavily, resulting in 14 serious inquiries, four interviews, and one job offer (that she accepted).

Basic Criteria Used by Recruiters

Many job hunters dream of attracting such attention (and get frustrated if they don't). However, not every candidate fits a recruiter's profile.

The Right Qualifications

First, you must fall into the search firm's specific area of specialization. (You may be a great R&D manager, but if the recruiter specializes in real estate, he or she can't help you.)

Recruiters also look at what Xagas calls "credential power." People who have earned degrees from well-respected schools, built careers with prestigious corporations or have an impressive track record of accomplishments are safe bets in this regard. Even if they ultimately turn out to be hiring duds, at least they had the objective qualifications to succeed.

FOR YOUR INFORMATION

DON'T FAKE IT

The quickest way to burn a bridge with a recruiter is to lie. If there's a problem in your background, be straight up about it and put your cards on the table.

Verification of Credentials

"You have to show honesty and candor with recruiters," says former contingency recruiter Rick Ehlers. "They need to know exactly where you're coming from."

Don't expect search consultants to rely strictly on your say-so. Good recruiters consider reference checking essential, so they use investigative researchers—often former police, military or FBI officers—to find out all they can about a candidate's background. This isn't paranoia; it's a question of survival. A recruiter's credibility is only as good as the candidates he or she presents, and a candidate who gets caught lying makes the recruiter look foolish and inept.

The Question of Fit

Identifying candidates with the right qualifications and verifying credentials is an important part of recruiters' initial screening function. However, headhunters usually spend the bulk of their time on the more subjective question of fit.

Reed-Belt estimates that she spends 25 percent of her search time on the issue of qualifications; 75 percent goes toward exploring fit.

In one case, she worked with the CEO of a financial institution who wanted someone exactly like himself to head up one of its newly acquired banks in Texas.

"He was a cautious man who reached decisions carefully, and it was important to him to find someone who would make decisions in the same way," says Reed-Belt. "He wanted someone whose behavior he could predict."

Thus, Reed-Belt asked prospective candidates lots of behavior-based questions.

"I wanted to hear specific examples of how they reacted in a variety of situations because I firmly believe that past behavior is the best predictor of future success," she says.

Another recruiter was asked to find a portfolio manager who lived in a certain wealthy Connecticut suburb.

"Basically, they wanted to know who rode in his car pool with him," the recruiter says. "Anyone who operated outside a certain ZIP code got screened out."

Personal Questions

At times, recruiters are placed in the unsavory position of becoming an employer's discriminatory arm. Under the guise of "fit," they may be asked to screen candidates on the basis of race, gender, age or other personal characteristics. In such situations, you may find yourself bombarded with a host of personal questions you don't understand.

A recent industry survey of recruiters' "favorite" questions included the following highly personal inquiries:

What are the values you were taught in your family?

How has your personal background (upbringing, schooling) influenced what you are today?

Discuss the importance of your job vis-à-vis your family and your faith.

Unfortunately, you have no idea what a recruiter plans to do with the information you provide in response—or, more importantly, what he or she may be looking for.

Ehlers believes that if you're interested in the position, you have no choice but to answer such questions openly and honestly.

"You have to remember that recruiters are often working with a very specific set of requirements that you know nothing about," says Ehlers. "They ask the questions they ask to determine if you fit those requirements, and if you don't give them that information, you'll automatically get screened out."

Whether you're talking to a recruiter or directly to an employer, it's best to plan ahead of time how you'll respond to personal questions.

If a question offends you, you can refuse to answer it. (Then, plan on finding another recruiter to work with you.) Otherwise, answer it, but do so judiciously. This isn't the time for true confessions, and, as always, put the best face on the truth.

For example, say you don't want to disclose that you're a devout Catholic, Jew or Methodist. You can tell the recruiter you have a strong religious faith (without revealing the denomination) that you always try to incorporate into your daily activities. Or, suppose you think the fact that you aren't married might work against you. You can indicate that you're very involved and committed to your family (meaning your parents and siblings), without necessarily saying "I'm still single."

The Recruiter-Candidate Relationship

Recruiters like to do extensive information gathering, but don't expect them to reveal much in return. Reed-Belt, for example, never divulges the name of her client and may not even explain anything about the position's responsibilities. As a result, it's difficult for candidates to customize responses and any efforts to do so may be quickly cut off.

"I'm looking for a person's core self, not someone who tells me what they think I want to hear," says Reed-Belt. "I'd never tell a candidate what client I represent."

Yee, however, has a different philosophy. Because she wishes to build a relationship with candidates, she explains what company and position she's recruiting for, and in return, she asks candidates to share their search information.

This approach has its risks, though. Once they know the details of an opening, some candidates contact the employer directly, thinking they'll generate more interest if no recruiter's fee is involved, Yee says.

Not only is this unfair to the recruiter, it's also unethical. Furthermore, it can backfire. One recruiter was so angry at a job hunter who went behind his back, he called the employer and had the candidate blackballed.

"Recruiters have relationships and agreements with companies," Ehlers says. "Candidates who go behind a recruiter's back may think they won't get caught but they almost always do."

Guidelines for a Positive Relationship

The relationship between a recruiter and a candidate proceeds more smoothly in an atmosphere of trust. You'll do your part to establish that trust by observing the following guidelines, especially with contingency recruiters:

1. Express appreciation for their interest.

2. Take time to learn about their practice and the market they serve.

3. Establish the ground rules for how you plan to work together and avoid duplication of effort.

4. If you agree to let recruiters shop you around, realize that you must live with your agreement. Don't undermine their efforts by going behind their backs.

5. Ask recruiters openly if they think they can help you (and how). In turn, share your relevant search activities with them.

6. Offer names of other candidates who may fit a recruiter's portfolio. In appreciation, they may set up more interviews for you.

7. Draw on recruiters' expertise. Ask them to brief and coach you for the interviews they arrange.

8. Be honest about your financial needs and goals. Since they receive a percentage of what they negotiate for you, it's in their best interest to get you the best possible financial deal.

9. Accept their role as intermediary. Until you're hired by an employer, their job is to function as a go-between.

Recruiter-Initiated Relationships

Recruiters who are actively seeking candidates for a specific position may initiate an unsolicited screening phone call. If you receive such a call, treat it like any telephone screening interview. Make sure that you have the privacy you need to conduct the conversation. In addition, you may want to check the recruiter's background, then call back. Like any industry, executive search has its fair share of charlatans. And if you're currently employed, you have a lot to lose with a recruiter who breaches confidentiality.

A manufacturer's rep was chagrined to discover that a recruiter with whom she'd interviewed had gone behind her back and told her present employer to expect one of his reps to leave soon. Since it was a small department, the manager had no trouble figuring out which rep was the culprit. Although she wasn't fired, the manager made her life miserable for the next several months.

Although the recruiter didn't technically breach the rep's confidentiality, he definitely sold her down the river in his haste to generate new business.

Candidate-Initiated Relationships

Other times, you may initiate contact with a recruiter in hopes that you'll be marketed to his or her corporate clients. In that case, your initial screening interview may take on a different flavor. Since there may be no specific job order with your name on it, you'll be interviewing to the recruiter's specialty area rather than focusing on what a specific employer wants.

Thus, Ehlers recommends contacting recruiters selectively, concentrating on those who specialize in your target industry or function. Your goal should be to build an alliance that will motivate the recruiter to want to help you. Sometimes, a little bit of personal information can go a long way in that regard.

Yee remembers working with a middle-market manager from Amsterdam who wanted to move to the United States to marry his girlfriend but wouldn't do it without a job.

"I'm a romantic," Yee says. "I fell for that."

So even though the market for credit-and-lending professionals (the manager's area of expertise) had bottomed out, she worked hard to repackage him—and found a position for him as a research analyst with a debt-rating agency.

But more than romantic visions inspired her. "He was a very articulate man with a lot of presence," Yee says. "I knew he'd present himself to employers well."

The Search for Presence

A candidate's "presence" is one quality that really makes recruiters sit up and take notice.

"Most hiring decisions are made in the first 30 seconds," says Xagas. "The way candidates project themselves—their aura, energy level and appearance—can make the critical difference."

It's not surprising that recruiters find a dynamic presence appealing. Once you've passed their initial screen, they still have to turn around and sell you to potential employers. And employers are impressed with candidates who make good self-presentations. A candidate who presents poorly often isn't marketable in the recruiter's world.

The Desirable Candidate

Are there other qualities recruiters look for that set a candidate apart? The St. Louis based *Fordyce Letter,* published by Paul Hawkinson, listed the following "water-walkers"—people who best meet a recruiter's needs:

☆ The Currently Employed. There are many reasons recruiters prefer people who are currently working. For starters, many employers have access to people who are unemployed because such candidates market themselves directly. Companies don't want to pay recruiters simply to cull through resumes for them.

In addition, although the numbers are diminishing, some employers still view unemployed people as damaged goods. Such hiring companies may request that a recruiter search only for employed candidates.

☆ Employees Who Are Anxious to Change Positions. Employers may want recruiters to go after employed candidates, but these managers may not be willing to make a job change unless they're unhappy in their current position. This ties into the next category.

☆ People Who Make Themselves Available for Interviews. Candidates who really want to make a change are more likely to be open and responsive when recruiters call and to make themselves available for interviews. It's hard enough for recruiters to get people together for a meeting without having to deal logistically with a recalcitrant candidate.

☆ Employees Without Many Job Changes. Recruiters prefer candidates with a stable, upwardly mobile career path. Frequent job changes are usually seen as an indication of either (1) performance problems, (2) an inability to fit in or (3) a lack of focus. Yet candidates' careers shouldn't be too stable, either. . . .

☆ Employees Without Too Many Years at the Same Job and/or Company. Employers assume that managers who have worked with the same company too long are either complacent or risk averse.

   Besides, "age discrimination is alive and well," says Xagas. "Companies still want young, energetic people who are really motivated to work."

☆ People Not Currently Responding to Classified Ads. "It's definitely a buyer's market for employers," says Xagas, who estimates that he receives 1,200 unsolicited resumes a month. In this climate, companies retain recruiters because they want to find someone who's really unique—and they don't expect to find that person through the classifieds.

☆ People Who Haven't Gone to Other Recruiters Recently. Again, a recruiter is only as good as his or her portfolio of candidates. Candidates may like the idea of working with several recruiters at once, but this won't do much for recruiters' credibility. And it raises that thorny question of who gets the fee (should the candidate get the job).

☆ Employees Who Have Secured Significant Time- or Cost-Savings for Employers. Recruiters can sell high performers easily. In fact, when a candidate's performance record perfectly matches the client's need to save time or money, the candidate basically sells him- or herself. This makes the recruiter look good.

☆ Underpaid Employees. Underpaid candidates usually are more easily enticed away from their current employers. And since their salary expectations may be lower (or more realistic), they're often more affordable. Plus, they give recruiters more negotiating room.

☆   Promotable Candidates. Most companies hire recruiters to find the best possible match. Having gone to this expense, they obviously want someone who will grow with them. Candidates who fit well with the existing culture are usually highly promotable. The expectation is that they'll become star performers within the organization.

Recruiters—Not for Everyone

Recruiters are a bonanza for some professional and executive candidates; for others, they're agonizingly unresponsive. If you fall into the latter category, it may simply mean that you don't fit a recruiter's profile or current set of needs.

This doesn't mean that you're unemployable. It just means an intermediary can't help you. In that case, you'll just have to work harder to sell yourself directly to employers.

"You're just the type we're looking for."

12

Customs and Protocol for Interviewing with Foreign Companies

I n the United States, we have an expression, "When in Rome, do as the Romans do." It's our shorthand way of saying: When you're in another person's country, follow their rules. But what happens when the Romans (or Japanese or Koreans or Swiss) are running businesses in the United States? Should we expect them to do things the American way, or should we view their corporate culture as a kind of mini-Rome in which we adapt to their modus operandi?

The answer depends primarily on two variables: (1) how Westernized the company and its executives have become, and (2) the employer's reasons for seeking American managers. In some cases, research will answer these questions, but other times, firsthand experience may be the only way to find out for sure.

For example, a customer service manager prepared for his interview with a Japanese electronics company by memorizing Japanese business expressions and practicing his bow in a mirror until he could execute it flawlessly.

As it turned out, the form of his greeting was perfect—but he delivered it to the wrong person. In Japan, the 90-degree bow is reserved for high-ranking Japanese politicians, corporate chairmen and royalty. Even worse, he bowed to a thoroughly Westernized executive who had been educated in the United States and had been residing on the East Coast for the past 20 years.

Fortunately, the hiring manager realized that the customer service manager was making a sincere, though misguided, effort to adapt to the company's culture. He shrugged off the error with a laugh.

In the meantime, we can learn something from the embarrassed candidate's mistake: When interviewing with foreign executives, make no assumptions. "It's easy to stereotype people who are different from us, but bear in mind that people don't always meet those stereotypes," says Mary Ann Lee, president of Workplus, a New York City career counseling firm. "Be open to the uniqueness of the situation and the person."

After all, some foreign executives retain the formalities of their native cultures while others adopt a more American style. Furthermore, your interviewer's native culture may be quite distinct from the overall corporate culture—or there may be more than one active culture within the same organization. At the Hong Kong Shanghai Bank, for example, there are Cantonese, British and American cultures all operating simultaneously.

Recruiter Florence Yee remembers working with two very different hiring managers within the same British bank. When the first manager—a friendly, open-minded Irishman—decided to go back home, he was replaced by a formal, aristocratic British banker. "Even people from the same country can have different styles," adds Yee.

Given the enormous potential for variations, will cultural research just lead you into a quagmire of stereotypes—or will it genuinely enhance your ability to understand and relate to individuals from a different country?

The Wise Use of Information

As long as you use the information you obtain wisely, country-based research should help you better manage your interview behavior and expectations. It would definitely be useful to know, for example, that in Japan, direct eye contact is considered a sign of disrespect, whereas in Mexico, it's considered an expression of openness and warmth.

Country-specific research can also help you avoid blatant gaffes. In a story that once made news headlines, Richard Nixon (in his role as vice-president) flashed the goodwill "A-OK" gesture to a Latin American audience, only to find out later that the gesture means "screw you" to them. (In his book, *Gestures,* Roger Axtell, a former international marketing executive with Parker Pen Company, does a wonderful job of chronicling such body language differences by country and body part.)

While you shouldn't try to change all your natural mannerisms to suit your interviewer's taste (there is something to be said for being yourself), heeding the following general rules can help you perform better in interviews with foreign executives.

Be More Conservative

This applies to your attire, demeanor and language. "The interview is a formal process," says Yee, who once was criticized for calling a foreign executive by his first name. "Informality doesn't go over well."

For this reason, avoid slang expressions "like the plague." They're inappropriate in a business setting and create an unnecessary communication barrier for nonnative speakers. Idioms such as "turning the tables" or "burning the midnight oil" simply may not be understood.

In one case, a candidate was trying to explain to a Chinese executive how he could use his extensive network to "get in on the ground floor." To this day, the interviewer can't figure out what building the candidate was talking about.

Don't Prejudge

We all bring biases to our interactions with people we perceive as being different from us. Often, the people we stereotype are very much aware of how we categorize them.

A nuclear engineer who had established a formidable reputation in his native India was acutely sensitive to (and frequently outraged by) the attitudes of many Americans he interviewed. Although he was in a position of authority, many candidates refused to listen to him or take him seriously.

He suspected this was partly related to his heavy accent, which he knew some people had trouble understanding, and partly to some deeply held prejudices against Indian people. So, although nothing was ever overtly spoken, the engineer automatically dismissed any candidates who appeared to feel uncomfortable with him or who made no genuine attempt to communicate.

The Mexican manager of an import-export company encountered similar prejudices. "Many Americans assume that Mexicans are lazy and uneducated," he says. "They simply don't know how to relate to someone who doesn't meet their stereotype."

Although you may not be able to reverse every inner prejudice and stereotype you harbor, you can consciously force yourself to be more open-minded in interviews. Rather than focus on differences first, try to establish a common social ground. You may discover you have more in common than you thought. And you'll surely listen better and respond more sincerely and empathically. This is a sure-fire way to build professional rapport and move the conversation forward.

Work Hard to Communicate

In the United States, we value assertiveness. But before you rush into your sales pitch, listen first for clues into the interviewer's facility with language. After all, what good is a great presentation if the interviewer doesn't understand English?

One candidate wasn't sure she was answering the questions of a German employer who had a very heavy accent. To make sure she was understood, she slowed the tempo of her speech and simplified her words. (Fortunately, she didn't fall into the common practice of talking more loudly.) She also posed lots of clarifying questions to ensure that she was, in fact, answering the question that had been asked.

It's really your responsibility to make sure your message is correctly received. When you accept this burden, you think *with* rather than *for* or *about* the interviewer, and rapport is definitely enhanced.

At times, this may require taking decided initiative. For example, a writer interviewing for a position with a French language school (which required fluency) could have earned some extra points if she'd asked to conduct the interview in French. This approach would have showcased her language skills and created a greater sense of a common bond.

It also might have changed the outcome—since the employer chose to hire a native-speaking, but otherwise less technically qualified, writer.

Watch Your Timing

Punctuality is valued by most foreign employers. To play it safe, show up as close to the scheduled time as possible.

Even if the culture tends toward lateness (as some Latin American cultures do), you'll seldom know the specific interviewer's bias. Better to show up on time (and have to sit around and wait) than show up late (and find out you're too late).

Too early doesn't look good either, as one Asian-American woman learned the hard way. When she showed up 15 minutes early for an interview with China Trust, the receptionist and the hiring manager found her earliness so disconcerting that they both mentioned it.

Keep Your Distance

Americans tend to operate (literally) at arm's length. Asians generally stand even farther back. But move over to Middle Eastern and Mediterranean countries, and things warm up considerably.

In any case, it's best to make no assumptions and take your cues from the interviewer.

"Just because someone has a Hispanic name doesn't automatically mean that you should kiss him or her," says Lee. "Wait and see what that person does first."

Manage Your Expectations

Americans like to move quickly, and it's easy for them to become frustrated with foreign executives who may be slower and more indirect.

In Mexico, for example, executives typically conduct business much more deliberately. They like to take time to find out who they're dealing with before they make any commitments. Lots of personal questions, especially about home and family life, are the norm. This also may hold true for Japanese interviewers, whose bias toward "community," makes them extremely sensitive to candidates' personal qualifications.

But rather than express your impatience, try to use the extra time and exploration to your advantage. After all, if you don't feel comfortable with the interview process, you probably won't feel comfortable in the day-to-day working environment, either. So participate wholeheartedly in discussions, then gauge whether you'd be likely to function well in that particular culture.

Don't Trade Ideologies

A computer scientist from Russia complained bitterly that candidates were more interested in talking with her about the fall of Communism than in describing their ability to program in "C" language.

"They were so anxious to discuss politics that they totally forgot we were in a job interview," she says. "It seems like I spent half my time steering them back to interview topics."

A South African owner of a Chicago manufacturing firm had a similar experience. While he was most concerned with a candidate's attitudes about customer service, interviewees often seemed more interested in protesting his country's apartheid policies—a stance that didn't do much to put them in his good graces.

Be Honest with Yourself

Many candidates are so anxious to find a job that they close their eyes to the realities of an opportunity.

By taking the time to understand how a foreign company's culture may affect your career, you'll be able to make a more informed decision.

FOR YOUR INFORMATION

EMPLOYERS HAVE BIASES, TOO

Certain cultures have longstanding biases against women, minorities, Americans, and so on. You may believe you're so good that you'll succeed despite these obstacles but don't count on it. "A lot of foreign cultures are very chauvinistic," says career consultant Mary Ann Lee. "An ambitious woman might want to think twice before she buries her career in one of those places."

"So much for salary talk . . . shall we move on to benefits?"

13

Talking Money

Satisfying and successful salary negotiations are a win-win game. Your goal should be to effect a mutually satisfying resolution between you and your future employer. You'll need several tools to master this art form: a strategy that suits your personality and the situation, a well-developed sense of timing, effective communication skills and the right attitude. First, though, you need to understand your role.

The Importance of Good Timing in Negotiations

At the beginning of the interview process, you're an unknown entity to employers. Because they don't know what you can do for them yet, early discussions of money are basically a screening device, a way to weed you out on the basis of affordability.

Establishing Value First

Your goal should be to keep yourself in the game longer. Even if the stated salary range is too low, the employer may be more flexible once you've established how great a contribution you can make. After all, labor is intangible; its value is in the eye of the beholder. After you've built value for your product, the company may be less resistant to the fact that it's expensive. People realize that quality costs—so first prove your quality, then name your price.

Questions about your salary requirements or history can surface as early as the initial telephone or human resources interview. At this point, you not only have no negotiating power, you may not even be talking to someone with the power to negotiate with you. Rather than box yourself in or screen yourself out, say that you're flexible, but need to know more about the position. (If the question is cast in terms of past earnings, convert it into a salary requirements question.) It's just too soon to raise a red flag over the issue of income.

You may not agree with my advice. After all, if the job pays too little, why waste everyone's time with further discussion? Simple: Because if you're a strong candidate and negotiator, the salary offer may improve significantly.

Think about the way people get to the point of buying something they can't afford, says Jack Chapman, president of Bernard Haldane's Chicago office.

Psychologically, such consumers go from thinking they can't afford an item to feeling they can't live without it, he says. As the urge to buy grows stronger, they move from a position of rigid neutrality to more emotional desire. They start looking for ways to shuffle their resources so they can afford to buy and come up with creative ways to justify the purchase.

The same logic applies to employment decisions. Get employers enthusiastic about your candidacy and they may become more generous. Therefore, your first and foremost task is to establish your value. Make employers believe that they can't live without the contribution you'll make to their organization. Since you can't do that until you know more about the position and the organization, you should always try to defer premature salary questions.

In Chapter 4, we talked about Patrice Becicka, a tax supervisor who lost her job when her employer closed its Iowa facility. Early on in an interview for a compliance position with AEGON USA, the company's human resources representative asked Becicka how much money she was looking for.

After naming some perfectly reasonable numbers, Becicka was told that they fit within the salary range but the company didn't usually like to start people out that high. Thus, Becicka was prematurely eliminated from contention for a position that truly interested her. (Ironically, she might have accepted the lower salary figure but was hoping for more.)

How might she have kept the discussion open longer?

Rick Ehlers suggests the following statement: "I can appreciate your interest in discussing salary but I'd prefer to defer the discussion until I know more about the position."

Another (more emotional) approach: "To be honest with you, I feel uncomfortable discussing money right now because I don't want to box myself in or screen myself out prematurely. First, I'd like to know more about the position and your organization."

In other words, focus the discussion away from the topic of money and onto the topic of job fit.

FOR YOUR INFORMATION

TIMING IS EVERYTHING

Don't discuss salary until there's an offer on the table.

Dealing with Persistent Questions from Employers

Employers are not always so easily persuaded to abandon the topic of money. When employers persist, Lee Hecht Harrison consultant Bob Maher recommends a "turnaround" strategy: "Ask them what range they've budgeted for the position."

This approach worked well for a $45,000-a-year computer programmer who was hoping for a 10 to 20 percent increase along with his job change. When asked his salary preferences, he responded, "Can you tell me what the job pays?" The interviewer replied, "We have a $45,000-to-$53,000 range." After that, all the programmer needed to do was nod and say, "That fits with my range."

But what if the range has been set too low?

You can say, "Thank you" and get up and leave; or you can get defensive and protest that you were making a lot more than that at your last job.

A better approach, though, is to reach for your homework and say, "Are you aware that similar positions generally pay in the neighborhood of $_____?" This strategy depersonalizes the situation, while also probing why the employer has set the range lower than industry standards. Knowing the employer's budgeting rationale can tell you a great deal about the organization.

Diversionary Tactics

Later in this chapter, we'll talk about how to anticipate objections and prepare justification statements. But for now, your task is simply to understand the employer's position and stay out of premature salary negotiations.

Sometimes, you can do that directly. Having received a disappointing response to your turnaround question, you can follow up with another query: "Can you tell me how you arrived at that number?"

This strategy directly explores the employer's needs and priorities, which positions you to build value for your candidacy and thereby "up the ante." You can then easily return to a sell mode in which you continue to establish your value to the employer.

Another good option at this stage is to express surprise at the figure but keep an open mind. Then, lead back into a defer strategy in which you "agree to disagree" until you know more about the position and the organization. So far, you still haven't tipped your hand on your salary requirements (although you may have implied your goal).

Some employers may find evasions irritating. If an interviewer really persists, you probably should name some numbers rather than risk further irritation. But what numbers to name?

Here's a situation when doing your homework can really pay off. Express realistic expectations and needs by using salary surveys as a basis for your requirements. This will also convey to the employer that you know your value in the marketplace and are seeking it.

If the employer casts the question in terms of your salary history, though, you'll have to take a different approach. One option is to distinguish between past earnings and future requirements by saying: "I can tell you how much I was earning at my last employer, but until I know more about this position, I really can't tell you how much I'd be looking to earn here."

This response serves two functions: It disarms the employer by complying with the request, yet at the same time, it establishes a distinction between your past history and your future desires.

If you think you were underpaid in your last position, you may want to convert the "salary history" question into a worth statement. Rather than just state your final salary, make a "calculated disclosure" that reflects your entire compensation package, advised Maher.

Such a strategy could have worked well for the computer programmer described earlier who was hoping for an increase from his $45,000 annual salary. By calculating in his 401(k), pension and profit-sharing earnings, he could easily (and honestly) have told recruiters: "Last year, my position was worth $52,000."

FOR YOUR INFORMATION

FRINGE BENEFITS ADD UP

Consider the total salary package. "Fringes" such as health care coverage, vacations, retirement and profit-sharing plans can add 25 percent to a worker's salary.

Still, making such "worth statements" early on can be hazardous, Maher concedes. They may force you into negotiations before you've had a chance to display your value.

Usually, it's wiser not to reveal your previous earnings at all, says Ehlers. "What you made before may be totally irrelevant," he says. "You could be talking apples and oranges."

For example, a real-estate professional earned nearly $80,000 a year plus perks doing site selection for fast-food companies. But when the real-estate market collapsed, there simply was less need for this professional's skills. In keeping with the laws of supply and demand, he needed to determine a more realistic financial objective.

"It's your responsibility to research the marketplace and make some determination of your value to that marketplace," Ehlers says. "Then convert the past earnings question into a realistic dollars-and-cents figure."

Another possibility is to "agree to disagree" on the issue of salary. Just indicate flexibility and a desire to learn more, then revisit the question later in the game when you have a stronger negotiating position.

The Moment of Truth

You've learned about the position and established your value, and the company genuinely seems interested. At this stage, a question about salary usually is a precursor to a formal job offer and the beginning of direct negotiations.

The time to defer is over. Now your goal is to get an offer on the table you can look at together. This time, in response to the question, "What kind of money are you looking for?" you can employ a new "turnaround" strategy with the statement: "Make me an offer."

Some employers may comply with your request immediately, or take some time to think about it. If a formal offer arrives in the mail or over the telephone, request an in-person meeting with the hiring manager to discuss it.

"It's too hard to read cues over the phone from someone's tone of voice," Ehlers says. "You need to look them in the eyes to pick up visual cues. Besides, it's harder to say no to someone face-to-face."

Other employers will say they need some financial information from you before they can formulate an offer. This can be an ideal time for a "worth statement," but precede it with a reiteration of your selling points. These will remind the employer exactly why you should be hired.

Once you know an employer really wants you, your first impulse may be to request the sun, stars and moon. Try to resist. Instead, name a figure that, based on your research, genuinely reflects the fair market price for your employment services.

An office supply company asked a senior systems analyst to produce two numbers before making an offer: the actual numbers on his pay stub and his "wish list" numbers. When he said "mid-50s" to the latter request, he was prepared to justify his desire with salary statistics he'd gleaned from a Source EDP study of what people in similar positions earn. As it turns out, the company met his "wish list" figures without asking him to defend them.

Right Associates' consultant Jim Kacena suggests naming a higher number that leaves room for the employer to cut your request back. This is similar to what Nelson, Harper's Dennis Huebschman refers to as "leaving some wiggle room."

Still, you must always anticipate potential objections and prepare rationales for what you want. Atlanta career counselor Mark Satterfield has identified three of the most common objections employers voice to high-end requests:

1. Budgetary constraints ("We don't have the money").

2. Your salary history ("You were only making $_____ in your last job").

3. Peer pressure ("No one else at your level is making that much").

In each case, try first to understand the employer's resistance, then prepare your justification. This usually requires an open mind and some sophisticated "mouthwork."

A sales rep who interviewed with a Delaware pharmaceutical company wanted $47,000 plus quarterly commissions, but the vice president of sales offered less.

She countered with, "Why do you feel my offer won't work for you?"

The manager explained that under the "old regime," others often were compensated along the lines of her demand. But the firm had discovered that when the base was too high, reps weren't as motivated to perform.

Understanding the situation enabled the rep to prepare a solid justification for her request. First, she encouraged the VP to recognize that some of her peers were still being compensated under the old system, so breaking precedent needn't be a concern.

Then, she focused on her personal situation. For her, it would be demotivating to take a pay cut, she said. If motivation was the issue, then she'd be far more motivated by the knowledge that her paycheck matched her worth. Because she was an experienced salesperson, she didn't need to prove her value; she just needed to get the company to agree to pay her according to the standards used for its more experienced and committed sales reps. In the process, she illustrated the power of her sophisticated negotiation skills.

Says Mark Satterfield: "Always remember that your goal is to reach a mutually acceptable resolution, not to squeeze every last penny out of the company."

Kacena agrees: "Negotiate as a friend and equal, seeking a resolution that's fair to both sides."

One easy way to do that is to express enthusiasm and appreciation for the offer. This helps establish a context of commitment and trust from which to work things out.

FOR YOUR INFORMATION

GUIDELINES FOR NEGOTIATION

CareerLabs counselor Linda Bougie recommends the following general guidelines for all salary negotiations:

1. Be flexible.
2. Concede minor issues.
3. Dramatize your concessions, not theirs.
4. State your desires in terms of their benefits.
5. Look for suitable areas of compromise.

From a practical standpoint, it usually makes sense to negotiate in order of descending levels of importance. For most people, this means starting with actual base salary. After that, you can discuss performance bonuses, commissions, benefits and other perks.

Negotiating Styles

In general, your negotiation strategy should reflect your personality and work style. Some people choose a passive negotiating strategy. This approach selects out one area of concern (usually salary) and (nicely) asks for more by questioning, "Is that the best you can do?" without making any specific demand.

Should the employer express an openness to your desire for more, you must be prepared with your demand, and a justification for it. On the other hand, if the employer expresses an unwillingness to bend, the game is over. Discussion ended.

Another, somewhat more assertive, approach relies heavily on the techniques of clarification and silence. In this strategy, you go through the employer's offer on a point-by-point basis, clarifying each item on the list. Your response might sound something like this:

I'm here to accept your offer, Mr. (or Ms.) Employer. But before I do, let me make sure I understand it completely:

1. You're offering me $55,000 per year. Is that right?
2. I'll be reviewed annually with a standard cost-of-living increase, but no merit raises. Is that correct?
3. You have a 401(k) plan with a 50 percent matching policy?

By pausing silently after each clarification, you can play on the employer's cumulative guilt to get more without ever asking.

Jack Chapman in Chicago also advises using silence as a negotiating tool. By repeating the figure, he says, you let the interviewer know that you heard the offer and are thinking it over. But your body language conveys that you're not entirely happy with it.

The outcome, Chapman claims, is usually a concession to your unspoken demand for more. However, if you'd rather ask for what you want than guilt-trip an employer into providing more, try another, more direct, negotiating style. This approach requires a clear understanding of your financial and emotional needs.

Richard Keyster, a risk/loss manager who was laid off after more than 20 years with Aetna Life and Casualty Company, benefited from such self-knowledge when a central Illinois insurance company offered him a job. On learning that the package didn't include a company car, he remarked innocently, "I'm used to having a car." To his surprise, the company returned to the bargaining table and immediately offered one.

Often, though, it takes a little more effort to get what you want. Reviewing the employer's offer carefully with an eye toward potential holes often helps. Rick

Ehlers remembers working with a national sales manager whose "sticking point" was relocation costs from Chicago to the East Coast. The executive brought in quotes from real-estate agents in both cities to justify a $15,000 salary increase. He got it.

Obviously, playing "hard ball" isn't recommended unless you're prepared to say 'no.'

"You definitely have to know your bottom line and refuse offers that won't meet your needs," Kacena says. "But that doesn't mean you have to negotiate with pistols. You never want to demand a concession or deliver an ultimatum."

It's rare, but occasionally offers are withdrawn during the negotiation stage. A retail marketing executive who kept asking for "more, more, more" discovered this the hard way. After two weeks of greedily nit-picking his prospective employer, the firm decided (based on his negotiation techniques) that it had made a mistake and rescinded the offer.

Obviously, this candidate took his strategy too far and alienated the employer. By sending an "I'm-not-going-to-be-happy-here-unless . . . " message, he set up a win-lose situation. And he lost.

Actually, the conflict over money may have reflected a deeper emotional issue. In his previous job, the candidate had been vice president of marketing. The new position didn't carry the same title, which to him represented a step down the career ladder. Perhaps he sabotaged the salary negotiations because he couldn't own up to the real issue at hand.

Remember that net worth and self-worth aren't the same thing. Confusing the two will only hurt your effectiveness. Rather than take low offers as a personal insult, view them as a challenge to your negotiation skills.

When an executive outplacement firm approached Rick Ehlers with a lowball offer, he used humor to push the numbers higher. "You don't want a professional," he said. "You want slave labor." The recruiter laughed and upped his offer.

Is there ever a time not to negotiate? You should always ask for things you feel are important to your career satisfaction. Many candidates mistakenly assume that salaries are preset and, therefore, nonnegotiable. This can become a self-fulfilling prophecy. If you don't ask, you usually don't get.

"Don't be afraid to negotiate because you think an employer will withdraw the offer," Kacena says. "In fact, most employers expect you to negotiate. Don't surprise them too pleasantly by backing off."

On rare occasions, however, employers may make offers that are music to your ears. Recently, without any prompting whatsoever, an industrial psychologist extended a dollar offer that was more than double my (unasked) asking price. While I didn't protest ("Oh no! That's way too much!"), neither did I feel the need to negotiate further.

Instead, I said, "Thank you. That's fine." And I shut up.

"I should have known there was something fishy when they offered me unrestricted use of the company jet."

14

The Wheel Comes Full Circle—Evaluating Job Offers

W hen a private Chicago hospital was forced to lay off 250 members of its health care staff, a surgical nurse found herself unexpectedly pounding the pavement. Fortunately, it was summer, which meant her MBA and MSN graduate school programs weren't in session. This gave her plenty of time to job hunt, and less than one week later, she had her first job offer.

The offer wasn't perfect. Although the money and job responsibilities were virtually identical, the benefit package was a problem: It provided very little tuition reimbursement, whereas her previous employer had paid 100 percent. By accepting the offer, she could ensure her ability to pay the rent and put food on the table, but it would mean the collapse of her many career goals.

Thinking it through, she realized she had four choices:

1. Try to negotiate a higher salary to compensate for the lesser benefits package.

2. Accept the offer and give up on school.

3. Accept the offer and keep on looking for other opportunities.

4. Turn the offer down and continue job hunting.

The first option (negotiation) was her first choice, but she doubted the hospital's pay scale could be stretched $15,000 higher. She also knew she could never permanently give up her educational goals, although she realized she might have to postpone them for awhile. That left her with two choices, both of which involved continuing her job search. It simply became a question of whether to do so as an employed or unemployed person.

There are advantages and disadvantages to either decision. If she accepted the position and kept on looking, it would (1) be unfair to the employer who hired her in good faith and (2) slow her search down, since it takes time and energy to learn a new job.

Yet, if she turned the offer down, she had no guarantee that she'd be offered another position anytime soon. This would create financial pressures, and she'd probably end up delaying her education, anyway.

Does it matter that she received the offer within her very first week of job hunting? Should we write this off to "beginner's luck" or read it as an indication that the laws of supply and demand are on her side?

The question leads to us to another option (which is, in fact, the one she chose):

5. Stall the employer for time in order to check out the job market.

For her, this meant directly contacting every Chicago hospital to determine their need for surgical nurses. Then, armed with a little more feedback, she was better able to decide whether to risk the wait.

Many candidates mistakenly believe that an offer must be accepted on the spot or it will be withdrawn. Rather than fall into this trap, express your appreciation and enthusiasm for the offer, then ask when a response is needed.

Most employers will give you a week to think it over. You may not need that much time. Perhaps you just want to "sleep on it" overnight, to make sure your questions have been answered. Or you may want to talk it over with your partner to make sure your family can live with your decision. Many professionals can't accept a job offer without first consulting the other people it would affect.

For example, an Indiana-based marketing manager wanted desperately to move his career into the international arena. His dream job finally came through, but it was in Ohio and his wife, a tenured university professor, had no desire to relocate. After many long discussions, they decided to live with a commuter marriage to keep both careers on track.

On the other hand, when a tenured journalism professor at an Illinois state school decided to accept a nontenured position with a prestigious private East Coast college, she didn't want to live apart from her husband and two children. So her husband liquidated his private law practice and started job hunting on the East Coast, knowing that legal jobs weren't plentiful there. Not surprisingly, it took him six months to find something suitable.

In another case, a Houston engineer turned down a higher paying sales engineer's job in Atlanta because his girlfriend didn't want to move.

Whether a job requires a move overseas, across the country, or simply from the suburbs to the city, you must consider carefully whether the sacrifice is worth the effort.

FOR YOUR INFORMATION

RELOCATION GUIDELINES

To decide whether to move for a new job, recruiters and relocation experts suggest the following guidelines:

1. Investigate the new area thoroughly. Make sure you see what you're getting into and that the city is a livable place for you and your family.
2. Determine how the new city's cost of living compares with your current situation and consider whether your salary will be adequate.
3. Evaluate whether the job opportunity is worthwhile. Don't move just to move.

When an accountant who lived in a Chicago suburb interviewed for a management position with a well-known restaurant chain, executives expressed a concern that his long commute into the city would interfere with his job responsibilities. Being single, the accountant decided to eliminate the obstacle by moving into a downtown high-rise. Before he made that move, however, he should have asked why a simple commute that thousands of people make every day would be a problem.

He may not have asked but he found out, anyway. Once hired, he was expected to start work at 6 A.M. every day of the week. Not only did he routinely put in 12-hour days, his job involved meeting hourly deadlines every single morning and then working straight through lunch.

"I didn't realize that I'd have to turn my whole life over to this job," the accountant remarks ruefully. "But that's what it's become. I don't have time for anything else, including looking for a new job."

Unfortunately, many candidates are so anxious to accept a position that they close their eyes to the messages an employer sends. During the interview process, the restaurant chain sent many signals that unrealistic demands might be placed on employees. Yet the accountant ignored the red flags and accepted anyway.

He was put through a rigorous selection process, including four interviews with different managers in different locations and an extensive battery of personality and aptitude tests. That's all standard procedure, but the fact that he was asked to personally coordinate the logistics of this complicated interview process should have made him wary. At the end of each meeting, he was given the telephone number of the next person to contact and instructed to schedule an appointment. Since each executive on his list was inordinately busy, he ended up literally spending weeks tracking down interviewers.

Then, after the fourth meeting, the subject of testing was introduced. The accountant amiably agreed, but then he heard nothing back for two weeks. Finally, he followed up with the human resources director, only to find that the group had "dropped the ball." No one even knew if a hiring decision had been made.

Apparently, his call prompted them to take action, because he was offered the job a few days later. But the company let him know that (1) he was coming in on the high end of its pay scale (message: don't expect any more money from us); and (2) that it doesn't usually hire from the outside (message: you'd better be worth it).

The way an employer treats you during a job interview is usually a good indication of how well you'll be treated as an employee.

When Jerry Hannigan received his first job offer, he was annoyed that the employer extended him an offer on Thursday and wanted an answer by Monday. "Employers have to realize that this is an important decision in someone's life," says Hannigan. "I needed time to think about it."

Had he been more excited about the offer, Hannigan might have been less concerned about the short timetable. But a second red flag went up when the employer refused to let him meet his prospective co-workers. When Hannigan wasn't allowed to "check the employer's references" this way, he knew he couldn't work at the company.

Timing often plays a critical role in your decision-making process. You may find that compromises you're unwilling to make in the beginning become more acceptable after you've realistically evaluated the job market—and vice versa.

In June 1992, Lana Steinman lost her training position with Packaging Corporation of America during a general layoff. Since this was her third layoff in 12 years (one company went belly-up and another was sold), she knew how to deal with the situation. To support herself during the transition, she started looking around for interim consulting positions and hooked up with several firms.

The following February, Steinman interviewed for a training position with a health-care products manufacturer near her home in Lincolnshire, Illinois. The job sounded promising. She knew she'd enjoy the work responsibilities, liked her prospective peers and was very enamored of the close location.

She heard nothing from the company until mid-May, when she was asked (as is standard in training) to do a presentation for the CEO, president and vice president of human resources. Her presentation went well and she was told that a decision between her and another candidate would be made the following week. By mid-June, she still hadn't heard anything. Reviewing her conversations with company executives, she realized that their failure to answer her questions about their training budget and resources indicated a lack of commitment to the position.

In the meantime, her consulting practice was blossoming and Steinman was reconsidering her decision to seek permanent employment. Although she'd always chosen job security first, her experience over the preceding 12 years had taught her that security is rare in the current American workplace.

Finally, she decided to commit herself to self-employment. So she called the health-care company to withdraw her candidacy—only to find that they wanted to offer her the job. "I had this moment of panic when they made me the offer," Steinman says. "Was I doing the right thing? Should I choose the safe route and accept the position?"

It only took a moment of soul-searching to come up with the answer.

"How much security can there be with a company that isn't committed to the job or the department?" Steinman says. She decided to keep on looking.

Periods of transition are almost always stressful. But they can also be opportunities to grow. For many laid-off executives, this means reevaluating needs, values and priorities to develop new directions.

When an architectural marketing professional lost her job, she realized that her former employer had actually done her a favor since she'd never really liked the work. She decided to change careers, but first she needed more skills. Her strategy was to take another marketing position that enabled her to go back to school and build some new credentials. Although she never told her new employer she was planning to be "two-year employee," in her mind, she'd made a distinction between short-term and long-term goals.

The marketing professional's actions display a new self-directed mentality in the workplace. People no longer expect to commit their entire work lives to one employer. Companies may lament this new "what's-in-it-for-me" thinking among employees, but it's really just a matter of "turnabout is fair play." Since employers no longer make lifetime commitments to their employees, they can no longer expect that kind of loyalty in return.

When an employer and a candidate decide to work together, they should do so because the partnership is mutually beneficial. Anytime the relationship stops benefiting either party, there's cause to terminate the contract.

People with a more survivalist "Depression-era" mentality have trouble with this new value system. They remember vividly what it means to be poor (and, in some cases, have passed those memories in the form of values along to their children). They still feel that people should be grateful just to have a job.

Ironically, most companies are looking for employees who really want to work specifically for them—people who can commit to their unique missions and goals. By knowing what you want (and actively seeking it out), you do both sides a favor and ensure a more productive and satisfying work partnership.

This insight doesn't develop overnight. It takes time and effort to understand yourself and how you best fit into the job market. Few people are willing to engage that process. Jerry Hannigan is an exception.

After being laid off from AT&T, Hannigan sent out more than 1,000 resumes, generated 76 interviews, and received several job offers. It has taken 15 months.

Many people think he's being too picky—that he should compromise. Having waited this long, Hannigan is loath to do so.

Currently, he's considering an offer from a microwave transmission company that recently restructured, hired a new management team and is gearing up to enter the international arena. Hannigan thinks there's a good market for the product, the career path is great, the money is right and the people seem smart and nice. But until he sees the final offer on the table, he plans to keep on interviewing. (Too many offers have already fallen through.)

In fact, he has two interviews pending next week—proof positive that he's still a viable candidate. The hardest part, he admits, is keeping himself psychologically revved up. He feels his age creeping up. (He'll turn 50 this year.) And, he'd like this part of his life to be settled.

But he wants to make sure that the decision he makes is the right one. His career depends on it.

Interview Log

s you arrange for interviews, keep careful records showing the date of the interview, who the interview was with, and any impressions you had after the interview. The following pages can be used as your personal interview log.

INTERVIEW LOG

INTERVIEW LOG

INTERVIEW LOG

Index

No matter where your career is headed, one source will point you in the right direction.

National Business Employment Weekly

Turn to us whether you're looking for a new position or to improve your present one. We'll not only provide you with hundreds of nationwide and regional job opportunities, we'll help you with expert career advice. From letter and resume writing for the job seeker to negotiating and networking strategies for the seasoned professional, National Business Employment Weekly is your source. So, no matter where your career is headed, make your next move toward success by picking up the National Business Employment Weekly at your newsstand. Or get the next 12 issues delivered for just $52 by calling toll-free...

800-535-4800

3GDX

Call toll-free 800-535-4800
or fill out this coupon and mail to:
National Business Employment Weekly
Box 9100, Dept. W, Springfield, MA 01101

❑ Yes! Please send me the next twelve issues, my check or money order for $52 is enclosed.

Name

Address

City

State   Zip

SPECIAL BONUS!

RECEIVE ONE FREE ISSUE!
NATIONAL BUSINESS EMPLOYMENT WEEKLY

No matter where your career is headed, the *National Business Employment Weekly* points you in the direction of career success. Whether you're looking for a new position or to improve your present one, you'll find hundreds of nationwide and regional job opportunities—highly paid executive, professional and technical positions—available now. Send in the coupon and receive one free issue and you'll agree that NBEW is the nation's number one job search publication.

☐ YES. Send me a free issue of *National Business Employment Weekly.*

Name _____

Address _____ Suite/Apt. _____

City _____

State _____ Zip _____

Complete and mail this coupon to:
Dow Jones & Co., Inc.
Attn: H. Magill
P.O. Box 300
Princeton, NJ 08543-0300

Offer good for a limited time, and only in the continental U.S.

© 1994 Dow Jones & Co., Inc. All rights reserved. **3UNX**

FOUR WEEKS FREE!
THE WALL STREET JOURNAL

☐ YES. Send me four weeks of *The Wall Street Journal* to enjoy free. At the same time, reserve an additional 13 weeks (17 weeks in all) at the trial rate of $44. That's the regular price of a 13-week subscription, so my first four weeks cost me nothing. Note: Offer good for new subscribers in the continental U.S. only. Limit: Only four free weeks of *The Wall Street Journal* per household.

Name _____

Address _____ Suite/Apt. _____

City _____

State _____ Zip _____ Sales tax may apply.

Complete and mail this coupon to:
Dow Jones & Co., Inc.
Attn: H. Magill
P.O. Box 300
Princeton, NJ 08543-0300

Offer good for a limited time, and only in the continental U.S.

© 1994 Dow Jones & Co., Inc. All rights reserved. **28WR**